HOLY ISLAND

A Lenten Pilgrimage
to Lindisfarne
by James W. Kennedy

Foreword

IN COMMENDING this book to the reader, I wish to take advantage of the analogy which Dr. Kennedy pictures in his title for Lent. If Lent may be described in the form of a Holy Island, then this book may well be regarded as the ship which will enable one to visit it, and my foreword as a form of launching.

This is a sturdy little ship, built on long-tested lines. The builder has traveled back and forth between the mainland and Holy Island often enough to know both the joys and the dangerous cross-currents of the passage, but it remains a voyage he loves.

I wish you the same inspiration that I have had in reading this book. Were you to remember that I am writing seriously, then I might risk saying, "Bon Voyage!"

Holy Island is one of the most helpful devotional books that has appeared in recent years. It goes out with my prayers for God's blessing on all who shall read it.

Horace W.B. Donegan, *Bishop*

Saint Barnabas' Day
June 11, 1958

Preface

THIS book makes no pretense of originality or of presenting earth-shaking ideas. There is nothing new in it, for all of it has been said over and over again by many men in many books. But repetition is one of the laws of learning, and the same concepts expressed in different periods of time from a fresh point of view have added, if not to our total knowledge, at least to our grasp and more complete assimilation of that knowledge.

I am indebted to an article which appeared in *The National Geographic Magazine,* October, 1952, page 547, for my initial interest in Lindisfarne—one of England's Holy Islands. John E. H. Nolan wrote of his "Pilgrimage to Holy Island and The Farnes" and provided a wonderful picture story to go along with it. In preparation for my own pilgrimage to this historic holy spot, I read *Guide to Holy Island,* by John W. Halliday, published by Andrew Reid and Co. Ltd., Newcastle-upon-Tyne, 1951 edition. I wish to credit both these sources for whatever is descriptive and historical in this book concerning Lindisfarne.

All this vicarious pilgrimaging to Holy Island through reading was made real when, at last, I set foot on the hallowed spot and knew for myself what such a pilgrimage can mean. It is in the mood and remembrance of several such visits that I write this book, especially the quiet of early mornings, when the tide was out, the birds were making small noises, and from far away came the first faint sound of the tide rolling in. On Holy Island I realized that *Tomorrow Is Already Here.**

May this book help you, too, make your Lenten pilgrimage vital.

James W. Kennedy

On Holy Island
Eastertide, 1957

*The title of a book by Robert Jungk.

6

O Lord, God, when tensions mount and fears plunge icy fingers into our hearts, hold us steady and keep us from panic, for we know that thou art our God, who cares for us and art ever with us, and we need not fear or grow tense. As we declare our faith in the good God revealed in Jesus Christ as each morning comes, and as we face the day's turmoil and unkindness with thee consciously present, help us to walk in faith each new hour; through Jesus Christ, our Lord.

A Word about Islands

ISLANDS have always been fascinating, and still are. It is very tempting when one is buffeted by life in the world or when one is confused and wearied by life's grim realities, to dream of an island apart from all the world's noise and strife. Perhaps one can actually flee to an island, in fact or fancy, always remembering the words of John Donne, who has made us forever sure that "No man is an Iland, intire of itselfe; every man is a peece of the Continent, a part of the maine. . . ."*

No one can be an island or live on an island completely cut off from the life of his fellows, for one would soon become ingrown and unproductive, living artificially. But we can make pilgrimages to one, actually or in our mind, and can designate any time or place of apartness as his Holy Island of retreat and spiritual renewal, provided we do not remain there too long. Therefore, to inspire and direct such a seeker, who, in the very midst of life's rush, needs a quiet refuge for a time apart to keep the meaning of life in proper focus, *Holy Island* was written.

This book is an analogy between an actually existing island, once made holy by those who lived there, and the mental image of an island to which one can make pilgrimages at any time, to gain wholeness and true perspective.

Devotions, XVII.

Note: The use of "man" and "men" and "he" is the generic term which includes both men and women.

Off the Northeastern coast of Great Britain there is a group of small islands dear to the hearts of all English Christian people since Saxon times. As the Flying Scotsman roars along the Northumbrian coast on the way to Edinburgh, between Beal and Berwick-on-Tweed the passengers can catch a glimpse of the nearest of these islands, unless a "sea fret" mists over the coastland. For centuries the largest of this group of islands, known as The Farnes, was called Lindisfarne, from the words *lindis,* the name of the expanse of tidewater one must cross to reach it, and *fahren,* which means a recess or place of retreat.

It was from this very spot that St. Aidan, St. Cuthbert, and many other Christians carried the light of the Gospel to England from A.D. 635 to 875, until the Danes came and destroyed the first tiny thatched church and slew many of the island's inhabitants. Since that long-ago time, Lindisfarne has been known as "Holy Island," holy to the memory of those devoted and courageous saints of God.

In the eleventh century a Norman church was built there, and the mission station flourished again. Although this ancient church is now in ruins and the North Sea no longer keeps a lonely saint company on some sea-washed rock, pilgrims still visit there and keep his memory alive. The legacy of the centuries on this tiny island remains to inspire all who, in this twentieth century, seek for a place of withdrawal for quiet reflection.

All of us need periods of withdrawal from time to time far removed from the turmoil, pressure, and hurry of the world, to get our bearings straight in silence, and to hear God speak to our special need. This seagirt Holy Island of Lindisfarne is an ideal analogy for such a retreat. It is actually cut off from the mainland for only a few hours at a time, at high tide, twice a day, and then connects again with predictable regularity.

Any period of apartness for refreshment can be likened to a Holy Island, whether it be a season within the round of the Church year—like Advent, Lent, or Ember Days— a conducted retreat or quiet day, or one's own private devotions. Those who are in the world, and who must of necessity live uncloistered lives, need a quiet place where their souls can catch up and be refreshed for return into the thick of life. One never remains for long on his Holy Island. The length of stay is dictated by the need.

All who wish may use Lent as a Holy Island and find themselves both cut off and accessible, both in the world and apart from it, practicing the rhythm of the spiritual life. Any season of the Church year, a summer vacation, a fleeting crossover in a moment of crisis, or a daily quiet time, can become a time of apartness for a long or short look at the interior life, and can be for anyone a Holy Island in space or time.

Think, then, of such a Holy Island of apartness where we can be shut off from the world for a time of quiet with God, for learning more about him and his way for us, at last to return to the world refreshed, strengthened, and straightened, better able to find wholeness and completeness within, fulfilling the purpose of our lives in God's plan. In this way anyone may find an island which does not separate us from the mainland of the world, but helps fit us for living in the world.

Lent comes once a year and can be used as a Holy Island where we take time to go apart and ponder afresh

10

the age-old theme of the love of God as revealed in and through Jesus Christ, and seek new ways as to how we can more fully share in that love.

As pilgrims, then, move on toward Holy Island, seeking directions for a way over and what to do once you are across, as Lent unfolds day by day.

Merciful Father, forgive us for all our neglect, luke-warmness, undisciplined thoughts and actions over the swift-passing days. At this moment of beginning a season of special prayer, study, and bodily discipline, give us the desire to be made clean and strong within and to give ourselves earnestly to the labors and care which will bring our desires and thoughts and feelings into one with thy will for us. This day we make our covenant with thee and ask for strength and guidance to mend, to give up, and to grow, through obedience to thy Son, Jesus Christ our Lord.*

*All prayers are from the author's prayers in the syndicated series "Prayer for Today," and are used by permission of the National Council of the Churches of Christ in the U.S.A.

ASH WEDNESDAY

Satan's Power Underfoot

LEGEND says that when Satan raised his giant battle-ax against Heaven's gates, God's shaft of lightning struck it from his hand. The flaming ax fell into the North Sea and was changed into the thousand-acre isle of Lindisfarne. Through the centuries this bit of lore concerning God's victory inspired those who lived on, or visited, this island, to keep Satan's power underfoot.

One of our special spiritual needs is a place like this Holy Island, where we can wrestle with the downward pulls which beset us and would conquer us. The battleground need not be a gloomy vale of tears and darkness, but a holy place of joy. And the disciplines of the fray do not demand "farewell to alleluia," for, above the noise of battle, the trumpets of God's victory sound. As good and evil struggle for the control of our lives, two weapons come to hand for the fight, namely, fasting and prayer. We go to Lindisfarne, the Holy Island, first of all to conquer the temptations which so quickly, continuously, and easily beset us, and to strengthen and refresh our spiritual lives.

Lent is the kind of Holy Island to which we make pilgrimages with joy, not sadness. Whatever we do on our brief retreats to Holy Island, the mood of our stay must not match the ancient gloomy precedent of such a season, stemming from the sixth century.

When the Lombards invaded Italy, about A.D. 568, all Christians were called on to observe a special season of fasting and prayer; but the invasion lasted so long some of the special supplications used became fixed in the liturgy of the Church and remained to give Lent a sad and melancholy face. By the ninth century there was actually a service, widely used on the eve of this penitential season, called "Farewell to Alleluia."

But when the pages of church history are turned even further back, Lent is found to have been a joyful time when alleluia was the accepted theme and worshipers stood for the prayers to show their joy, because of Christ who loved them enough to give his life for them and who had redeemed them from their miserable condition of ignorance of what God was like.

"There is something wrong with our religion if it is all taken up with our Lents of respectable self-improvement. Our faith must be outgoing, to the down and out and to the up and out. We should seek self-improvement only in order to serve the Church's mission better. Lent is a time of self-denial and opportunity" *(Forward Day by Day, 1968).*

Fasting is a weapon for Christians to use against the temptations and vanities of the world, and all the other evils which bedevil us without ceasing.

"Turn ye even to me, saith the Lord, with all your heart, and with fasting . . . and rend your heart, and not your garments, and turn unto the Lord your God: for he is gracious and merciful, slow to anger, and of great kindness. . ." *(Joel 2:12-13).*

"When ye fast, be not, as the hypocrites, of a sad countenance: for they disfigure their faces, that they may appear unto men to fast" *(Matthew 6:16).*

Only God sees us on our Holy Island as we "fight the good fight with all our might" against spiritual foes. Therefore, we need no ashes heaped upon our heads or sad countenances to show our inner sorrow and what we are striving to do about it. Before we win any other spiritual victory we must win out against the great temptation, "the luxury of cheap melancholy," which is only a superficial display of sorrow and fasting with no roots or wrestlings to it.

"When thou fastest, anoint thine head, and wash thy face; that thou appear not unto men to fast, but unto thy Father. . ." *(Matthew 6:17-18)*.

O Lord, when the light of thy truth shines in our eyes, let us not blink and turn away. Help us to look squarely at whatever is revealed—our touchiness over some fancied slight, our resentment over even a hint of criticism, our condemnation of others, our insensitiveness to another's need. Make manifest thyself as the light that shines into our darkness so that we may see.

THURSDAY

Fasting as Abstemiousness

Look more closely at the meaning of fasting. While the severe and extreme practice of fasting was common on Holy Island in the distant past, when St. Cuthbert and his brother monks could give themselves over to it as their life work, it must be a tool fashioned to meet the challenge of today's life in order to become of value for Christians in this modern world.

Fasting is a much larger word than it is usually credited with being and may be used devotionally in at least four senses: one, as abstemiousness, a bodily discipline; two, as a means of increasing the pace of spiritual growth; three, as taking a firmer grip on faith; and four, as a more deeply and permanently dyed evidence of spiritual stature.

Fasting as a bodily discipline means *abstemiousness*. The body must be kept under if the soul is to grow. We pamper and overindulge the body in almost every conceivable way until at last we must call a halt (on our own initiative or by a doctor's orders) and seek to exercise more control over bodily appetites and either over-exertion or sloth. For those who indulge inordinately in food and drink, fasting means moderation. For one in bondage to a bad habit, fasting is the strenuous labor of breaking that habit. When a day or a season of fasting is observed, when the body is disciplined by telling it what it shall have and do rather than letting it do the dictating, the fast is kept and we are better for it. The Church provides a table of fasts in *The Book of Common Prayer,* days "on which the Church requires such a measure of abstinence as is more especially suited to extraordinary acts and exercises of devotion." On fast days the body is deprived in order to benefit the soul. This can mean abstaining from meat, according to ancient custom; or it can mean abstaining from fish, if one is inordinately fond of it, as an exercise in self-discipline. Almsgiving is also to the fore, as one seeks to save in certain areas of unnecessary spending, even to the point of sacrificing something greatly desired, in order to give the money saved for use in spreading Christ's Kingdom, and to show our concern for all God's children.

16

Lent offers many chances for practicing such self-denial. It is much easier to fast during this season since it is the general practice of the whole Church, and many others are joining in. To accept certain needed disciplines, so that bodily matters will not interfere with nor dominate the affairs of the soul, is important for all. This involves abstinence and temperance: in eating, drinking, spending, and in every other area which has gotten out of hand or out of control. Such a fast means tightening up former laxity in such matters, giving up what is harmful, non-essential, or less essential, so that time, money, and physical strength may be used for more important matters. To fast in this sense means making more time for God, taking on whatever disciplines may be required.

O God, for another day, we thank thee; may its hours pass by swiftly, but not so fast as to leave us helpless in the flow of things; let the minutes and hours find us ready for the work to be done; help us make the most of the endless opportunities to serve and to love; may every contact this day bring new happiness and new knowledge; keep us near to thee through all the day, and, no matter what hours have been spent or remain to be spent, keep thou near to us.

FRIDAY*

A Quickening

FASTING as the means of *quickening spiritual growth* during a withdrawal to Holy Island, acts like a shot of

---

Observed in many churches as the World Day of Prayer.

17

vitamin B$_1$ at the roots of a wilting plant to give it new life. The season of Lent provides many stimulants for speeding up spiritual growth. Extra services of worship become small islands for frequent and quick visits, like the many islands, adjacent to Lindisfarne, labeled by such quaint names as Megstone, Crumstone, Little Harcar, and Glororum Shad. The monks of yore sought these isolated spots as places of retreat, even from the cloisters of Holy Island, as an additional discipline for aiding spiritual growth. Early celebrations, afternoon litanies, services of music, an open church offering sanctuary, and other opportunities for worship may be used for allowing one's soul to expand. We can find windows opening to a larger life through the words of worship—in the Bible or in *The Book of Common Prayer*.

One can also participate in a variety of study opportunities in certain neglected areas of the religious life, selecting from a rich store of serious reading matter designed for the season and for developing the interior life which is usually starved for just such fare. Most parishes give suggestions about books which can provide rich and stimulating Lenten reading. In some parishes Lenten Book Clubs are formed, where several persons band together for reading, discussing, and growing spiritually through sharing.

The pilgrim will check frequently to see that "this work [of spiritual growth] goeth fast on, and prospereth" *(Ezra 5:8)*. Fasting in Lent can mean, then, speeding up, getting a move on, realizing "the time is at hand" *(Revelation 1:3)* for stirring up our wills and for producing visible evidences of the answer to the confirmation prayer, "that we may daily increase in [his] Holy Spirit more and more."

Dear Father, we pray too often for ourselves and too seldom for others. Keep before us this day those for whom we should pray—the lonely ones to whom we might speak, the timid ones we might encourage in the Way, the hopeless ones who need a share of someone's hope, the unloved ones who need so much love.

SATURDAY

Grasp Faith More Strongly

FASTING is also used to get a *firmer grip on faith.* When we strengthen our staying powers, so that temptation does not pull us away from our intent, and never give up our striving to increase our spiritual stature and deepen our interior life, we are truly making fast, anchoring, that which has been given to us of the Way of life. But bodily discipline and spiritual growth must lead to another aspect of this third point, namely, to resist successfully the temptation to grow weary of well doing and chuck the whole business. When a bad habit has been conquered, we cannot cease our vigilance. When we have established a time of daily devotion, we must never grow lax.

Lent can be a time of stock-taking and concentration on getting a firmer grip on the essentials of Christian faith—and the frame of reference is the Apostles' Creed, especially as given in its summary form in the "Offices of Instruction." This creedal statement is prefaced by the words "I learn to believe." In Lent we learn to believe more firmly and completely in "God the Father, who hath made me, and all the world; in God the son, who hath redeemed me, and all mankind; in God the Holy [Spirit], who sanctifieth me, and all the people of God."

19

Eveylyn Underhill has given us a wonderfully compelling study of the Nicene Creed and its relationship to the inner life. Her small book of meditations, *The School of Charity,* is rich and vivid reading for those who base their spiritual life on a solid belief in God's revelation of himself in Christ, and his continuing presence.

Fasting reaches deep into our inner life and, in this area of holding more firmly to our faith, provides an anchor to windward, so that we shall no longer be subject to this ebb and flow of the tides of life, nor be "tossed to and fro, and carried about with every wind of doctrine" *(Ephesians 4:14).*

O God, we thank thee for the gift of speech, that we may communicate one with another about thee, and make known thy gift of eternal life through thy Son Jesus Christ. Help us to use our voices divinely; inspire and control our tongues. Gear our speech slow enough for wisdom, but fast enough to catch and hold attention; and give our words power enough to be convincing. So help us to further the coming of thy Kingdom, through Jesus Christ our Lord.

I LENT

Evidences of Spiritual Growth

FASTING is used to obtain *more deeply dyed evidences of spiritual growth and stature.* The lasting results, the outward and visible consequences of such a chosen fast, must indicate that those who have chosen it have been deeply and permanently dyed by their experience. If fasting has been freely accepted and truly kept, the color and tone of the spiritual gains will not fade under the glare of the noonday sun of testing and temptation.

Any season of fasting is kept in order to bring forth a more Christlike life. Such days apart in quiet, struggling with stubborn selfishness, remind of St. Cuthbert's Duck, which breeds on Lindisfarne and may be seen there all the year around. There is an analogy here between the forty days of Lenten discipline and the twenty-eights days the female duck sits on her eggs. During this time she eats nothing; she lives off her own fat. She fasts to bring forth more life. St. Cuthbert fasted in order to bring forth a more Christlike life. So must all who fast.

The acceptance of fasting in any form, and keeping that fast, whether to discipline the body, to get a move on spiritually, to hang on more tightly to one's faith, or to realize an unfading experience of Christ, makes unforgettable any trip to Holy Island; and the pilgrim returns to the world more alive, better nourished, calm and refreshed, able to make good "his first avowed intent to be a pilgrim" *(Hymn 536).*

Let our avowed intent this Lent be to fast from over-criticalness, from self-pity, from ill-temper, from resentment, from jealousy, from pride, from selfishness, from faithless fears, from worldly anxieties, and from whatever else dwarfs and hurts the soul. For such fasting leads to feasting on praise, on joy, on peace, on contentment, on love, on humility, on service, and on faith. Check your Lenten Rule to see if it covers all the disciplines of fasting.

Fasting, almsgiving, and prayer are inseparable and are needed to keep Satan underfoot, for he is always squirming and twisting to get free. If, like St. Cuthbert and his cloistered brothers on Holy Island, we are to hold to the disciplines of fasting and almsgiving, we must heed Christ's admonition to all pilgrims and wayfarers, "Watch and pray, that ye enter not into temptation" *(Matthew 26:41)*. For only so can this lonely warfare against rebellious self, which refuses to be denied without giving battle, be fought successfully, so that self is put in its proper place, and no longer blocks off God.

It is customary in some churches to set up a "Rule of Life" for the Lenten season. While this rule varies, it usually includes fasting, penitence, almsgiving, prayer, and devotional reading. Many disciplines may be used to equip the Christian for the exacting life he must live in the world. Among them are disciplines of moods and appetites, of the body, of thought, of speech, of money, and of time. But all demand the discipline of rising early enough for an unhurried communion with God, before the rush of the day's work begins. For everyone shall fail in all these disciplines if they attempt them in their own strength. (Adapted from the *Lee Abbey News Letter,* as quoted in the parish paper of Christ Church, Crouch End, London, *News From the Hill,* March 1957.)

Open the doors of our hearts, dear Lord, and enter in. Deal with what thou dost find of sin and contrariness, of discouragement and fear, of guilt and loneliness. Make peace in our hearts, good Lord, and send us forth with thy strength to face the day and not run from a single encounter, certain that thou art with us.

FIRST MONDAY

... And Prayer

THE monkish saints who dwelt on and peopled Lindisfarne gave themselves regularly to the discipline of prayer, as well as fasting. They prayed at set times in their thatched cathedral (replaced later with a Gothic structure, the remains of which are still standing); they also prayed at odd moments, each in his favorite cave or on his favorite rock. In prayer they found spiritual sustenance for a rugged life and spiritual power so contagious that all England was at last touched by it. They took literally Jesus' command "that men ought always to pray, and not to faint" *(Luke 18:1).*

Constant prayer was the secret of their holiness, and from such frequent, almost continuous times of prayer, came their love, patience, courage, and zeal which made Holy Island memorable. In this long line of saints and martyrs and humble men of God are many exceptional men who prayed on the heights. As one today looks on the life of those they know and on their own life, they realize how seldom most of us really pray. Even many of those who are willing to pray are seldom able to.

The atmosphere of prayer can be discovered on a visit to Lindisfarne, or by a walk through the quiet ruins of a holy place like Fountains Abbey. The spell of such places of prayer still holds those who walk there, surrounding them with a sense of God's presence. They are carried back through the centuries to the time when such an abbey was a flourishing place and men were happily engaged in productive, creative work, and in prayer. In such undisturbed spots apart from the world, in the atmosphere of stillness found in such a place as Fountains Abbey, it must have been easy for them to pray. Hours were spent on their knees. Indeed, apart from the necessary chores and requirements of living, prayer was their sole business. One still feels the very presence of God in such a place.

These ancient stones must be encrusted with the prayers of the faithful monks. That is one reason people still visit such places as hallowed ground and gain from them long-remembered inspiration. What a contrast between those saints of God and us today! They prayed constantly. We now so rarely pray at all. The monks must have had their moments of doubt and spells of coldness, but they kept everlastingly at it.

Certainly all the praying in England was not done by monks apart in hallowed spots, even at the height of the monastic age. Many ordinary persons knew how to pray then; and ordinary persons can now. Most of those who read this know in their hearts how faithfully they have attended church services, shared in the great prayers of the Prayer Book, and in private have said their own prayers with some degree of regularity. Look for a moment at public prayer, remembering John Keble's familiar hymn: *And help us, this and every day, To live more nearly as we pray*.

The real reason for coming together in corporate

worship is to respond in the deepest possible way to the Eternal God in whom we place our trust. However we come, usually immersed in the world of things, gradually our unpromising condition is transmuted as the service unfolds and we begin to respond to some aspect of Reality, some incitement of God, however dimly understood and imperfectly obeyed. In any humble response to the presence of God is the beginning of that love which manifests itself as hope and faith. As St. Ignatius said, "Contemplation [is] to procure the love of God." Real worship can change us by the presence of the living God revealed to us in Christ.

Many Americans have been brought up under the long extemporary pastoral prayer of the very informal Protestant service of worship and, even as children, were faintly disturbed by it. It was formless, graceless, repetitious, always "telling" God, quite obviously a technique for speaking to the people in the pews as well as to God.

The beautiful, time-tested prayers of the Prayer Book are like manna after all this. But the words of the liturgy can become so common and familiar that the responses in corporate worship are quite as meaningless as the extemporary, unrehearsed pastoral prayer.

But for both there can be an emptiness—in hollow extemporary praying and in liturgical routine droning. Everything depends on the worshiper's response to the God whom we come to worship.

There are so many mysteries in worship beyond our knowing, Lord. Let us be content with what we can know—that in thy presence we find peace and quiet, that life is sweet and to be lived to the utmost, that evil exists which can spoil it but that thou hast come to overcome it.

Help us to act on that knowledge. And may we leave the rest to thee.

FIRST TUESDAY

Prayer and Words

As we study the lives of those who have prayed through the centuries and read their contemplations, we are inspired to make our own practice of private prayer more continuous and fruitful. But as Thomas à Kempis wrote in *The Imitation of Christ,* "Truly in the day of judgment, we shall not be examined as to what we have *read* but as to what we have *done*. . . ." In *reading* the great devotional classics we learn straight off that these saints of God *labored* night and day to be more perfect pilgrims and instruments of the Divine Will.

Christians have always looked upon prayer as a *response* to the ceaseless outpouring of love and concern with which God lays siege to every soul. Prayer for them is always a response to the prior love of God. It is almost like standing before a closed door and finding God has been there all the time, waiting for us to open it and let him in. But prayer takes time and needs privacy. And yet the very depth of man's sense of need and desire will help him find a place for a time of daily quiet, apart with God.

Words are not needed. We do not even need to kneel. All we need to do is to realize we are in the presence of God and offer him our minds and hearts as receptive instruments. We may pour out our needs before God. We may offer another's needs to him. We may simply wait upon God. But we are seeking for God's will in order to do it. Preoccupation often makes it difficult to remove self from the center and let God be there. We find that prayer, which is usually thought of as an oblation (an offering of self), is also hospitality. Intercessory prayer means to offer one's own being for another for God to use as he wills.

What we are asked to do daily in prayer is to yield ourselves to God and no longer try to manipulate life for our own ends; to abide in him that his words shall abide in us—so his will may be done.

It is quite true that, for class instruction, prayer is often broken down into categories like adoration, confession, thanksgiving, intercession, and petition—and these are natural divisions; but what it all adds up to is that whenever we pray we must allow enough time with God each day to find the communion and direction which are the indispensable food and drink for our souls.

Grant to us all this day, dear Lord, enough sense to see what is right and to practice it, to recognize what is wrong and to avoid it, to yearn for and work for the best and happiest relationships with all whom we shall meet, and may "the trumpets that sound in the morning" for us be heard as far as we walk, speak, and reach; and, good Lord, keep us free from all narrowness, pettiness, and self-sensitiveness, so that thy joy may abound in us and touch others.

FIRST WEDNESDAY

Prayer in Private

PRIVATE prayer poses the same difficulties as public prayer. It seems to grow increasingly difficult for us to pray in the traditional way. We have less time and less privacy; we are too intellectual and too afraid of emotion, and we seldom pray, except in time of crisis when we do pray. And yet fewer psychiatrists would be needed to deal with our inner conflicts if the habit of prayer were better established in us and we prayed more consistently.

An intimate searching of our heart reveals a biting hunger for reality in prayer, even though we find many excuses and discouragements at hand for not praying either corporately or privately: "My heart is dry as dust."

Evelyn Underhill, who explored the depths of prayer and worship beyond even that which many "saints" experienced, maintains that "prayer and worship are not equivalent." Prayer "asks," she says, while worship "offers." Worship means "only God." Prayer means "without thee I cannot live." The pilgrim begins saying "without thee I cannot live" and ends knowing "only God."

Until mid-July, 1934, life was fairly routine for me. I was already ordained: I read the Bible daily; I knelt for my prayers, and my religious life seemed quite adequate. Then I had a serious airplane crash and almost lost my life. For many months I had no regular time for Bible reading; I could not kneel for prayer. About all I could utter when the pain was bad was, "My God." Or to say, "Thank God," when I realized I would not lose my eye or my leg. Or to cry inwardly, "Into thy hands I commit my life," when I had to face another operation or treatment. Prayer became for me an acknowledgment of God's nearness, God's goodness, and God's ability to do what was best for me. My entire prayer life was different because of this experience. So often we cry out for miracles of healing when all we need is to entrust ourselves to God's loving care.

Each day, John Wentworth, the vicar, went to the village church to say his daily office. Each day he would resolve to have a better prayer time. "Prayer today would be no dry wilderness. He would be able today to pour himself out in wordless adoration, without distractions, without encroachment, in perfect abandonment of will and libation of love. This was on his good mornings, but on his disastrous mornings . . . the whole business of intercessory prayer became no more than an arid discipline. Words, words, words. Why had he ever thought that they had any beauty? Each was as dry as dust as he forced himself on through them. Blast this toothache."*

Little things do distract, and yet we must persevere before the rewards of discipline come.

Prayer is more trust than utterance, more an attitude of heart and mind than of body. When Jesus heard the disciples plead with him, "Lord, teach us to pray" *(Luke 11:1),* he gave them the "Lord's Prayer." Did he mean for this formula to be repeated endlessly to be sure his followers would be praying correctly? Most assuredly not. In these words Jesus gave the substance, meaning, and technique of Christian prayer.

*Elizabeth Goudge, *The Rosemary Tree,* Coward McCann, Inc., N.Y., 1956.

"When ye pray . . ." *(Luke 11:2)* pray to this kind of God and remember to consider with him three things: his will, your bodily needs, and your relationships. When we pray, say "Our Father, . . . lead us" *(Luke 11:2-4).* Prayer is keeping in touch with God and making a commitment to him who provides guidance and strength and whatever else is needed for life.

Most of us who drop petitions in parish "Intercession Boxes" need to do our own praying as well and ask, "O God, show me what to do and give me the strength to do it," then wait for the answer. How can we take an unforgiving attitude when forgiveness is the only solution? There is an inner compulsion in us to mend broken relationships, but most of us are too proud to take the first step. God says, "take the step." And whenever we obey, the rift is soon mended, and we move on with joy.

Good Lord, send us such a measure of thy goodness that all our contacts may leave behind a bit of thy presence and glory. As the day moves from start to finish, keep us alert and ready to seize upon every chance to speak a good word in thy name. Let no obstacle frighten us; and help us to discern and minister to the need and bring out the good in each person we meet.

FIRST THURSDAY

Christ at the Center

ANYONE could make up a symposium on prayer, ranging from a simple poem called "A Prayer is Such a Sunny Thing" to one of Soren Kierkegaard's prayers, or one could make a thousand different interviews to find out how others pray, without gaining one single practical insight. We can never learn much about prayer until we begin seriously to pray and keep at it, even when nothing seems to happen.

On a visit to Kronberg Castle in Germany, I had a room near the tower clock which struck the hours and the quarter hours. Day and night the small tinkle called my mind and heart to prayer and I could almost put myself in the prayer pattern of those monks on Holy Island, where the monastic hours were filled with prayer and praise from Prime to Compline.

Some of the prayers of the saints remain to inspire and guide us today, such as the Prayer of St. Chrysostom at the end of the Prayer Book Service of Morning Prayer. But the greatest need is to take more seriously our own corporate and private prayer life so that we may pray more frequently and more perfectly as did the saints who knew God and lived obedient to his will.

John Keble set the goal: "To live more nearly as we pray." But first we must pray.

The reason the monks on Holy Island placed a rude sandstone cross at the very center of their community was to remind them that Christ must ever be placed at the center of each life. This Saxon cross stood for centuries, and even though the rough stone base is all that remains of the original today, it still bears mute but eloquent testimony to those who prayed there, and serves to remind those who pray in any place that Christ is at the center of their prayer life.

St. Cuthbert's Cross, planted deep in the heart of Holy

Island, and the Rainbow Arch of the ancient church still standing, remind pilgrims of the lasting beauty of the spiritual life and the place prayer plays in sparking life with contagion and power. The rhythm of each time of prayer apart on Holy Island is expressed in Sir Walter Scott's poem:

> *The tide did now its flood-mark gain,*
> *And girdled in the Saint's domain;*
> *For, with the flow and ebb, its stile*
> *Varies from continent to isle;*
> *Dry-shod, o'er sands, twice every day,*
> *The pilgrims to the shrine find way;*
> *Twice every day the waves efface,*
> *Of staves and sandalled feet the trace.*

Therefore, "pray without ceasing" *(I Thessalonians 5:17)* and maintain the rhythm of the devout life. Come to absorb from God, go to give to others, never forgetting that temptations and trials beset everyone without warning. "Sea frets" often quickly surround us, fogging our vision, and we need daily, frequent times with him. The rocks and caves which abound on Holy Island are symbols of the strength to be found in the hidden times and places of prayer. For those who visit their holy island and place Christ at the heart of life, life is a walking prayer. We can pray in any place—while waiting for a bus, while riding on the subway or in a taxi—for we can be alone with God any time we choose.

O Lord, this is the day which thou hast made, let us rejoice and be glad in it. When temptations come to yield to bickering tendencies and mournful complainings, let us remember thy gift of life and give ourselves to living it fully rather than spoiling and wasting it; so help us to honor thy Name through all this day and the waking hours of this night, and may our walk and words bring joy.

FIRST FRIDAY

Thanks-giving

On Holy Island prayer and thanks-giving go hand in hand. In addition to praying more regularly and faithfully, we must catch up on our thanks-giving and teach our negligent hearts to pour out alleluias for all the blessings of this life. Our lives are often in ruins, like the ancient Priory, with only a faint hint of the proper form and grandeur once in evidence. Through the practice of prayer and thanksgiving, we can be set on our way back to glory, like some valley of dry bones slowly reconstructed and reclothed with flesh.

The theme of thanksgiving runs through the Sacrament of Holy Communion and through all of worship, public and private, as a cord with binding power. Through thanksgiving we are bound more closely to him whom we worship, even Jesus Christ in whom we find this oneness fully expressed. It is in this experience that we find the very essence of religion, which is to bind God and man forever together so there will be no apartness.

Praise and gratitude and thanksgiving—expressed in "psalms and hymns and spiritual songs," in giving glory and in prayer, in endless alleluias, in creating beauty out of glass and stone and precious metal—have furnished the zeal for man's response to God all through the centuries. This is worship, a response to the "outpouring of the loveliness of God" *(St. Thomas Aquinas)*. The outward manifestation of thankfulness, gratitude expressed in the gift of self given in return for his unspeakable rich gift of life, especially his life in Christ Jesus, is also worship, seeking "only God."

Every act or feeling or thought of thanksgiving is filled with happiness and joy. When we catch the vision of God in reality and fullness, in the words of Bishop Serapion, "The very dust becomes happy in the contemplation of his Glory." Or, as the mystic Ruysbroeck puts it, "I must rejoice without ceasing, although the world shudder at my joy." Or, as Brother Lawrence discovered, even in the drudgery of the scullery his heart was so full of love and thanksgiving for Almighty God that the rattle of the pans became a hymn-tune and the swish of the water on the hard, cold stone an anthem in praise of him.

There is joy in thanksgiving—joy in God's creation, the wonder and beauty of it; joy over the fruits of the earth, symbolized and localized in bread and wine; joy over God's redemption wrought by Jesus Christ. No wonder the service of Holy Communion is called the *Eucharist,* which means literally "thanksgiving," and is bursting with offerings, alms, and oblations, as tangible evidences of Christian love. We can give without loving, but we cannot love without giving, of self and substance.

We are reminded of our debt to God and the need for the continual returning to give thanks in such words as the *Sursum Corda,* "Lift up your hearts. . . . Let us give thanks unto our Lord God."

As we pour out our hearts' alleluia, we "give thanks for

all men" and pray for "all who are in need," indeed for all mankind.

This spirit of thanksgiving and joy springs from faith and hope and must find expression in some act, some outward sign or manifestation of the inward thoughts and feelings. *Thank* and *think* are from the same root. The conscious recognition of God's good gifts fills us so full of thanks and gratitude our hearts overflow. There is always a spillover to thanksgiving.

But in the story of the ten lepers cleansed, we are reminded that only one returned to give thanks. Is that the usual percentage? What this story tells us is that it is easy to forget to be thankful. Therefore the emphasis on Holy Island is on thanks-giving. But there are those who think they have nothing to be thankful for. One helpful device, which has been the turning point for others in despair, is to write a thank-you note every morning to someone before the day's work begins. Even those who are at the bottom of despair have come up with names of persons to whom they can write thank-you notes.

Another good habit, when thanks-giving is difficult, is to attend an early morning celebration of the Lord's Supper. That is why pilgrims constantly refer to the Sacrament of Holy Communion, and seek to make their communions, for all who truly enter into eucharistic worship cannot [or should not] be indifferent to hunger, bad housing, children crippled by ghetto life, and other social and material evils.

Dear Lord and Father of us all, forgive our foolish ways; mend the breaks and relieve the tensions we have caused in our relationships; clothe our minds with wisdom so we may make a right judgment in all things;

*strengthen us to stand up against injustice; humble us to
the point of graciousness; and so fill us with thy Holy
Spirit that we may ever make known thy love and truth,
through our words and actions of thanksgiving.*

FIRST SATURDAY

Lips Not Kept Silent

ON a small rock or islet some hundred and fifty to two
hundred yards southwest of Holy Island, the foundations
of a chapel, supposed to have been used as a retreat by St.
Cuthbert, may be traced. The Venerable Bede of Durham
describes it in his writings: "A place more distant from the
monastery, surrounded on every side by the returning
waves of the sea." The chapel was very small, the dimensions being approximately twenty-four feet by twelve,
with walls two and a half feet thick. It was all he needed as
a place to celebrate the Eucharist. This site marked the
cell which the saintly hermit divided into two parts. One
part served as living quarters, the other as his prayer
room.

Times of worship enable us to take notice of those
special moments when thankfulness overwhelms us—a
wedding, a birth, a death (for the blessed remembrance of
that which cannot be lost or taken away). All such experiences of thanksgiving are times when mind and heart are
lifted up as an offering to God, and they produce a better
working interrelationship between God and us, between
us and others, between the cloistered and uncloistered
world.

Contrast the difference between the swelling happiness

of a thankful heart and the bitterness and aridity of an unthankful heart.

Thanksgiving is both general and specific. There is "A General Thanksgiving" at Morning and Evening Prayer. There are suggestions for special thanksgivings in *The Book of Common Prayer*. There is a prayer of thanksgiving at the conclusion of the Service of Holy Communion. These should be used more frequently, with a full consciousness of their meaning.

The doctrine of thanksgiving, fully embodied in the Eucharist, is an attitude of mind and an inner feeling, moving us to action. Therefore, "the personal response of the individual life follows the great rhythm of the Church's liturgical life. It too is Eucharistic" *(Evelyn Underhill)*. Because of this acute sense of thankfulness in his presence there ensues "loving subordination to God, a quiet acceptance of 'the sacrament of the present moment' as a major means of grace, whatever its form" *(Evelyn Underhill)*.

In thanksgiving, we find one of the secrets locked in the ruins of the old Priory on Holy Island, and we recapture some of the beauty of prayer and praise practiced by those holy men, whose hearts never ceased to pour out alleluias in thanksgiving to God. We should be so thankful for God's gifts that we take "the stuff of every-day temporal existence" and make it holy by offering it to God, "so that it may be accepted, changed, and become the life-giving stuff of eternal experience" *(Evelyn Underhill)*. This must be done not in the interest of the individual entirely, but in order to further the creative purpose of God, to open a channel for his Spirit, and so contribute to the redemption and transfiguration of life. "Each separate life of worship, whatever its outward expression, in so far as it is truly cleansed of egoism and bent upon God, is part of this one eternal Eucharistic action of the *Logos* incarnate in the world: and this fact strips the Christian life of prayer of all petty subjectivism, all tendency to mere religious self-culture, and confers upon it the dignity of the Real" *(Evelyn Underhill).*

We must be thankful for being fed on the spiritual food of his presence, for receiving sufficient grace to continue in the Christian fellowship and to live in the world. We must be most thankful for the gift to us of God's beloved Son and "pray fervently, labor diligently, and give liberally" to make him known. And he is made known as we live out in service the deep abiding thankfulness inspired by his love.

We thank thee, O God, for this day and the opportunities for growth and service it contains; keep us from muffing our opportunities to be kind; make us sensitive to the needs of others and desensitize us to the point where we do not mind little stings; in times of uncertainty let us lean upon thee and find the way to walk and the word to say, in harmony with thy will for us.

Second Week of Lent

II LENT

God's Graciousness

For those who pray, spoken or written prayers are not absolutely essential. But, to guide one's praying, a form of words is often helpful to cover more accurately the intention. Such prayers are available in *The Hymnal 1940, The Book of Common Prayer,* and in many excellent collections.*

Some years ago the National Council of the Churches of Christ in the U.S.A. began a syndicated feature called "Prayer for Today," with the intention of providing a brief, simply-worded guide for those who pray, which would point up one need each day. While the classic prayers of the Church will never be supplanted, our praying can be stimulated and clarified by the use of words in the modern idiom. That is why a selection of these prayers have been included in this book for the days of Lent. Each prayer is designed to speak to a specific moment or day in a person's life.

Of course, one prayer voiced silently or aloud does not mean one is praying. The praying actually begins when, by God's help, we begin to live out the intention of the words in a new life, reconciled to our neighbors, following the commandments of God, and walking more nearly in

---

*Two useful collections are: *Prayers New and Old* and *Prayers For All Occasions.* Forward Movement Publications, 412 Sycamore St., Cincinnati, Ohio 45202.

his unselfish ways. Only then will "the grace [the graciousness] of our Lord Jesus Christ, and the love of God, and the fellowship of the Holy [Spirit], be with us all evermore."

The Gateway to the ancient Priory on Lindisfarne has been restored, and all who gaze upon it or walk through it can see the splendor which was there in the beginning and gain some understanding of what it means to have one's life restored through prayer and thanksgiving.

So we pray and give thanks, on or off our holy island, for prayer to the Christian is a mandatory discipline which brings insight and courage in its wake. "If any man will do his will, he shall know of the doctrine, whether it be of God" *(John 7:17).*

Good Lord, help us to take some sin or carelessness that has not been faced, forgiven, and put away, and deal with it now in thy presence. Help us to face it honestly, confess it, receive forgiveness, root it out, and mend whatever was strained or broken by it. Help us to put on the glasses of thy presence and see things in focus, sharp and clear, and be no longer content with vagueness.

SECOND MONDAY

Litany of Life

HUNDREDS of pilgrims each year wade across oozing North Sea sands to visit Holy Island, or go over the causeway by car or taxi. This island center of early Christianity in Northern England lies in the churning sea, edged by sharp, rocky promontories and treacherous reefs. Some twenty-five small satellite islands dot the rough waters for several miles out to sea. About half of them are under water at high tide. As the tide ebbs and flows with unceasing regularity, it covers and uncovers the solid points of the rocky, smaller islands in The Farnes cluster, playing a "now you see it, now you don't" game.

The tides reminded the monks of the antiphonal form of the Litany with the exposed land "calling" the surging sea and the rushing waters coming in to "answer" it. Christian life is like this, visible and invisible by turns. The Litany, with its concern for all conditions of life, voices our petition and response. We go to our holy island to have this experience of ebb and flow of life, in the world, yet out of the world, exposed, then hidden, and we need a form to express the rhythm of worship. The Litany is one of the most ancient ways to reveal our needs and to ask for God's help.

The words of the Litany should "give wings to the earnest common prayers of the people." Cranmer translated, arranged, and composed this first service in English, based on the ardent devotions of the medieval church, making it comprehensive enough to cover the whole range of human need. Through Cranmer's skill, the incisiveness and vivid appeal of ancient phrases come down enriched and enhanced, but blunted of none of their poignancy and potency.

The petitions of the Great Litany are used by many worshipers, but do they remember any "wings" on those "earnest common prayers" as they pray them, and do the cries of "have mercy upon us," "deliver us," "hear us" come from uplifted hearts? The great words of petition and intercession are often empty of meaning. There is often no appropriating of the prayers by the worshipers and there is no heart in the responses, for we are not involved in them. Possibly this is because they are too general, or too extensive, or too familiar, or the very sound of them is too archaic for modern ears.

Even though the wide sweep of the Litany covers the whole range of human need and is really quite up-to-date, the quaint phrases often fail to touch us personally. Perhaps that is why the monks spent so many hours illuminating their manuscripts of the Litany so at least there would be something to look at to relieve the crashing boredom of its frequent use—*The Lindisfarne Gospels* is a good example of their art work. At least we are spared now from such superstitious sounding phrases as this one found in an earlier litany, "from ghosties and ghoulies and long-legged beasties and things that go bump in the night, Good Lord deliver us," although if one were to stay at an inn on Holy Island this phrase would be remembered in the creaking noises of the night, as the wind shakes doors and windows seeking entry.

Often during the reading of the Litany in a service of worship, the alternating solo and chorus drones on and some worshipers think again how seemingly pointless this endless repetition of words can be and how little of the love and truth of God are revealed in them. But at the very instant when such thoughts begin to distract and the wings of inattention threaten to waft us away, our minds are alerted to the meaning of some petition sounding loudly in our ears and our consciences are pricked, for example, by such words as "from all blindness of heart" or "from pride, and hypocrisy" or "from envy, hatred, and malice" or "from battle and murder, and from dying suddenly and unprepared."

At such points one really prays the proper response, "We beseech thee to hear us, good Lord." Taken one by one, these marvelous little summaries of human need cease to be liturgical only and become devotional and specific, timely enough to needle us to the quick, provided we are conscious of their meaning and grab them for a longer look as they move across our minds.

The Litany need not be automatic and dull routine discipline or a mere duty to perform, but it can be a relevant word to one's present, ongoing life, a moment of true insight on one's knees.

The birds which haunt The Farnes have taken possession of every pinnacle and exposed rock. Visitors often find hundreds of these birds wheeling and slipping, zooming and dipping to within an inch or two of their heads. They swarm overhead and punctuate the hours of devotion like some litany of motion. The phrases of the Litany often come alive, seemingly aimed at us like the Holy Island birds diving from the circling heights straight for one's head.

Such petitions as "give to all thy people increase of grace" have often brought to us fresh and strong knowledge that all words in worship are drone and weary repetition until we become involved in them, until the sound of them comes as a message from God to us direct, and until we offer our own heart's desire along with the words. Then worship comes alive in a definite response to them and we are ready to be involved and to bring forth *fruits* of the Spirit.

"Involvement" is a word full of meaning on Holy

Island, strangely enough, and means for us to enter fully into what we pray for.

Dear God, we want to know what to do this day under the remembrance of yesterday's trials and the knowledge of today's temptations. We surrender our worried way to thee and ask for faith enough to know and strength enough to do thy will. Keep us close to thee and make us ready to go forth.

SECOND TUESDAY

The Point of It All

TRYING to encompass all the Litany each time it is said is like trying to use all the recipes in the cookbook each time a cake is baked, or like trying to store up enough spiritual power during one trip to Holy Island in Lent to last a whole year. But letting a phrase or two catch and hold us can spur us to action in areas of faith and love, can be God's spoken word for each one to hear and heed, according to their need. Take that portion which has come alive for many—the prayer for an increase of divine grace to hear, receive, and act upon God's Word.

In order to hear and receive God's Word "with pure affection," our love for him must be uppermost. Jesus said, "If a man love me, he will keep my words; and my Father will love him, and we will come unto him, and make our abode with him ... and the word which ye hear is not mine, but the Father's which sent me" *(John 14:23-24)*. And again Jesus said, "He that is of God heareth God's words" *(John 8:47)*.

44

We are called to expose ourselves to the Word of God, as St. Cuthbert did when he let the icy salt water swirl over him as he prayed. As we come to worship we expose ourselves to the Word of God, hungry for the truth of God, eager to respond to his presence in whatever way he prompts—while standing and praising him with thankful hearts in song; while sitting quietly waiting for his Word to pierce our hearts and penetrate and lodge in our minds; or while kneeling humbly to ask his forgiveness and his mercy.

There is nothing quite so useless as a pencil without a point. Every home should have a pencil sharpener, for children and adults alike are always breaking the points on pencils and discarding them. There are piles of point-less pencils in most homes put away in some drawer or box, forgotten and lost. A pencil sharpener could put them back into operation. In order to get down to a new exposure of the graphite core, the wood must be shaved off, and this process must be repeated at intervals throughout the life of the pencil.

Any time apart on Holy Island acts on our faith and love very much like the sharpener on the pencil, the Word of God giving point to both. The disciplines of obedience to God's Word shave off the wood which wraps up our love and faith, exposing both to view again, ready to begin writing with sharpened points a new page in the story of our lives. When we are close enough and attentive enough to hear his words, we begin to be shaved down to the action edge.

God's words can rub around most of us for a long time, like the blades of a pencil sharpener, before anything happens and a sharp point is produced, not because their cutting edge has dulled but because we are not shoved into the midst of them far enough for close contact. God's words can shave off the outer parts and reveal what is underneath only when we are held close to the sharpness of them.

Prayer and worship, even the words of the Litany, can lure people to go all the way in yielding to the love and truth revealed in God's words, until at last they are touched and changed by the presence of God, restored to usefulness, like old pencils made new. No wonder we call such islands of experience "holy."

That phrase in the Litany just considered may have caught and pushed some minds all the way into the pencil sharpener, and God's Word may have come as judgment upon their attitudes, and the petitions may have become for each person a prayer for the increase of grace *for me* to hear meekly God's Word, *for me* to receive it with pure affection, and *for me* to bring forth the fruits of the Spirit. When anyone can claim this prayer is *for me,* it is God's call to one individual to share in the drama of salvation, for at that moment he is alone with God on Holy Island, knowing no other, and the cry "have mercy" is a response to his divine love received the moment we are open to it.

Only as we *"hear* meekly" God's Word, and *receive* it with "pure affection," utterly given over to it, and hold to what we know of him which has come through the Word, with love, can we prevent his words from passing us by and leaving us as empty, graceless vessels to be overcome by evil in one way or another.

O God, help us to see as far as we can and then trust thee with all beyond sight; we ask to know thy will and way, and wait for thy strength to do and to follow; so may we live our best for thee from day to day.

46

SECOND WEDNESDAY

Two Gathering-Up Points

THE analogy of the pencil sharpener stirs up the whole question of redemption from ugliness and uselessness and pointless lives. Is not salvation from human sin, through repentance and soul surgery, a painful and continuing process? God's redemption is the daily renewing of our worn-down points, making sharp and useful the potential always present—as the sharpener reveals the graphite in the pencil.

Often one runs into those who have been disillusioned by some experience and have turned hard or bitter or cynical. They are suspicious of everyone and are always thinking or asking, "What's his angle?" "What's in it for him?" crediting no one with a generous or unselfish motive. For the understanding and growing Christian there is always a triangle, not an angle: a desire for completion—the self fulfilled in God and others—with all three angles of the triangle opening on the center from which the love and faith of God operates.

For the Christian, human relations are not like the disconnected dots at the end of a line, indicating there is no more to come, or that something has been left out, but they are like base angles at the bottom of a triangle representing us and others, with God at the top. The founding fathers of our country knew about such a triangle and placed it at the center of human contacts. The pyramid of the Great Seal on a dollar bill has the eye of God at the top. We carry it around in our pockets, when we can. We should also conspicuously carry it around in our minds, hearts, and relationships—each one of us, with God over all.

There is nothing quite so useless as a hidden faith, without vision or staying power, is there? There is nothing quite so pointless as love which never moves beyond the circle of self-concern, is there? There is nothing quite so pitiful as a potential son of God not revealing the image of God which is in every man, is there? So Holy Island beckons all men to come apart and deal with these matters without delay.

Be not, therefore, insensitive to the great words of the Litany, for they, too, are of God and stand ready to reveal to us some portion of his love and truth and the way to appropriate both in whatever phrase of it strikes home. If we take Jesus' word for it, that God accepts us and loves us just as we are, once we have come to our senses and have cried, "Lord, have mercy upon us," then we are enabled to accept ourselves without running away, without always holding the cynic's mask over our faces; and we can even love ourselves in a constructive way and begin to amend our lives according to his Word.

Close and continuing contact with the living God in worship, fasting, and prayer relaxes the tension and anxieties, sloughs off pride and the attitude of self-sufficiency, breaks the power of sin, and saves us from ourselves. For God helps us face ourselves as we really are and furthers the innate desire within to move from there. This is the beginning of our redemption.

There are two gathering-up points to take away from Holy Island: one, continue to face self in the presence of

God; two, strive to come as close to him as the pencil to the sharpener and ask for the point revealed to be made ready for use, however painful or oft-repeated the process.

Never forget that really to pray any part of the Litany with understanding and benefit to oneself and others, requires us to stay with it until the point is made, following the example of the saints who lived on Holy Island, whose dominant characteristic was humility.

O Father of mercy, in the grip of darkness of sin we turn to thee in sorrow, with an earnest desire for a forgiven and cleansed life; make us whole again; help us to find solid ground in our mire of helplessness and disobedience, and make us worthy to follow the trail thy Son blazed from earth to thee.

SECOND THURSDAY

On Looking Within

THE Longstone Islet Light is a beacon tower which shines in the darkness on the treacherous point. Its great foghorn sounds as the fog rolls in, and it has saved many a vessel from "the Farnes' fangs." This massive column of red stone, towering above a rock base, has been called Grace Darling's lighthouse ever since one wild September night in 1838 when the frail daughter of its first keeper made a heroic rescue.

There is nothing more treacherous than shoals hiding underneath innocent-looking water, especially when fog blinds one's eyes. Inevitably when we cross to our holy island to be alone with God, the light flashes and the foghorn sounds, warning us to look beneath the surface of self to confront the dangerous places hidden there. This is self-examination, or taking a long look within.

When John the Englishman and Jean the Frenchman first met in a crowded railway station, in Daphne du Maurier's novel *The Scapegoat,* here is what happened as John tells the story: "Someone jolted my elbow as I drank, . . . and as I moved to give him space he turned and stared at me, and I at him, and I realized with a strange sense of shock and fear and nausea all combined, that his face and voice were known to me too well. I was looking at myself."

Most men feel a little like John as they catch an accurate glimpse of their counterpart, Jean, and are filled with "a sense of shock and fear and nausea all combined" at what they see. It is not often we ever get such an honest and startling reflection of ourselves.

However, Lent may be used as a mirror in which we may peer as we make a sober reappraisal of the self we see, not selfishly or morbidly as the center and despair of existence, but in relation to other men and to the whole wide world which surrounds and influences life.

Our face is a baffling mask when we first look at it. Behind the face lies our mind, which is a "junkshop and a confused utopia," especially when we try to discern and catalogue our most cherished habits and beliefs as we look within. But any self-study pursued with courage and patience, without dodging the truth, will bring some order out of this welter of confusion, if each one "turns a stream of fresh and full thought upon their stock notions and habits" and penetrates the mask which for so long has hidden their real selves.

Most of us are blind to our true selves. We are like the blind man in St. Luke's Gospel sitting by the side of the Jericho road begging alms. We sit in the darkness of our blindness begging alms, when we should be busy at whatever it takes to regain our sight.

Those spiritually blind need inner sight as well as outer sight, before they are able to stand upright again and move along without stumbling. The bump into a "double" in a railway station is most unlikely, although if we wish, we can see ourselves as we really are any time we care to look.

Note St. Luke's story of the blind man *(18:35-43)*. No one knows how long this man had been taking his place by the Jericho road begging for alms. It is known, however, that one day, when the blind man's entreaties reached Jesus' ear, he stopped and asked him, "What wilt thou that I shall do unto thee?" And the blind man (whom St. Mark called Bartimaeus) replied eagerly with hope rising in his heart, "Lord, that I may receive my sight." And Jesus said unto him, "Thy faith hath saved thee." And immediately Bartimaeus received his sight and was blind no longer. He arose and followed Jesus, glorifying God. Imagine, if you can, the miracle of restored sight and the joy of a man, blind for so long, now seeing again, in visual contact with life.

The conclusion reached from Luke's treatment of the story is that Bartimaeus really wanted to receive his sight back, in spite of the fearful changes this would mean in his life, all of which he probably did not foresee. No longer would he have the "security" of blindness, living off the work and sympathy of others. Now he would have to earn his place in society and take responsibilities, with no

51

excuse for his failures to measure up. But his desire and his faith in Christ were real, and because of this the miracle took place. What happened beyond the moment is not known, but would it not be hard ever to lose sight of such a miraculous change in one's life?

O God, guide us aright and lead us toward inner peace and rest; and be in our hearts and minds to enlarge them and keep them ever-growing; and, O God, as we go into the day's life, guide us and help us to walk unafraid until tomorrow comes.

SECOND FRIDAY

Inner Blindness

WE often fail to see that blindness goes deeper than the clouded eyes which surgery can sometimes cure, although physical blindness quickly wins our sympathy. It is the blindness all around and within which escapes our notice *(Psalm 115:5)*.

Certain questions for any self-study emerge as the story of Blind Bartimaeus is pondered and applied to moral, mental, and spiritual blindness. Since Luke had been healed of inner blindness by Christ acting through the Apostle Paul, it must be assumed that the answers to these questions were implicit in his version of the blind man healed by Jesus on the Jericho road. Does not sight require us to walk away from a beggar's mat into the discipleship of Christ, away from the uncharitableness, away from racial prejudice, away from snobbishness, away from the old life into a new life, as evidence of the

52

changed condition of one who is blind no longer?

Most of us are afflicted with an inner blindness to truth, to human need, to our own uncharitableness and unlovingness, and to our own prejudices, a blindness which most of us do not want cured because in a peculiar way we actually enjoy it, for it gives us a way to rationalize our miserable and shabby conduct. Even if we are aware of our blind spots and recognize what is happening to our relationships because of them, we are sometimes afraid to face the light, for we really don't want to regain our sight. Perhaps even when we do see the need for more accurate insight and really want to be changed, we do not have sufficient faith in Christ to ask and mean, "Lord, that I may receive my sight, for I am ready to do whatever is necessary to see things whole again." All who fail to ask remain sitting by the Jericho road.

Inner blindness to one's real condition of habits, beliefs, and attitudes is a prevalent disease, originating frequently in our fear of life as well as our fear of death, which causes us to close our eyes and shut out the world with all its perplexing problems and responsibilities, thinking thereby to escape them, or that by doing nothing everything will be all right. But responsible Christians cannot neglect forever facing truth about themselves, feigning blindness.

During this Lent, then, open your eyes wide and take a look at yourself in the midst of the present world, so that you may more fully express God's will for your life. All who take a look and see themselves as God sees them, must avoid any degeneration into morbid introspection and deeper withdrawal into the dark caverns of self. This Lenten stocktaking can result in a more Christian and healthy outlook and inlook, provided those who participate hold themselves to the unpleasant but rewarding task until they have been given a few honest glimpses of what restored sight can mean.

Blindness is revealed in many ways, but perhaps most clearly in our cherished habits and attitudes so long unquestioned we cannot evaluate them correctly. We are often blind to all but what we want to see. A person was once disturbed when the incident of the whale swallowing Jonah was mentioned as having no primary bearing on the point of the story, namely, our obedience to God's commands. That person had always believed in the literal inerrancy of Scripture, but had never read the Book of Jonah, nor heard it read, and when it was suggested that he read it, he refused. At the other extreme of blindness is the man in the Graham Greene play, *The Potting Shed,* who had a vested interest in atheism through his published works, and who refused to see any evidence of God's existence and power, even when the evidence was placed on his own doorstep.

When such areas of blindness are probed, whether in beliefs of habits, attitudes or relationships, thoughts or feelings, motives or morals, we come up with conditions in ourselves which need our patient and concerned attention until sight is restored, by God's help. A serious self-study will uncover the blindness inherent in the vain and selfish woman, the ruthless businessman, the cruel and possessive "loving" mother, the blatant-mouthed masquerader who is really a shy person underneath; the congenital liar who is dreadfully insecure, the lieutenant who passes himself off as a major, the superman concept so widely evident which has wrecked many lives in every age, or whatever else we see as we look in the mirror at the reflection of our own true self. Most of these types can be seen in Terence Rattigan's sensitive play, *Separate Tables*. Here, the imagery of separate tables in a British hotel restaurant is used to depict human loneliness, isolation, and blindness, and the need for understanding and fellowship. The play shows what an honest facing of these several conditions of blindness can do to change them, as, one by one, most of the characters wake up to themselves and are on their way to recovery at the final curtain.

Dear Lord, open our hearts and minds to a new understanding of thy word; give us courage, calmness, and confidence for facing whatever lies ahead this day; and keep us in the straight and sure way of thy peace, through our Savior Jesus Christ.

SECOND SATURDAY

Windows Opening

In making a self-study many of us who call ourselves Christians may find we are blind to what being a Christian means. A Christian is one who believes that God cares and that through the Incarnation (the coming of Christ) and the Atonement (the Sacrifice of Christ) he has shown that he cares supremely about all, knowing them at their worst yet still caring for them and giving to them. Therefore, if we really see this we will respond with love toward him who loves us so much, and with love toward other human creatures whom he loves along with us. A Christian holding this belief can never subscribe to the shrug-of-the-shoulder philosophy or the couldn't-care-less attitude, but at all times will seek to know the truth and live by it.

When an honest appraisal is made at last—and this takes a lot of courage—building signs of the beginning of things coming a bit more right can be seen. We less quickly blame others for whatever happens to us. We more readily see and emphasize the good in others. We more humbly realize we do not know it all and are not perfect, or hopeless, and so begin to learn.

One of the great things Christ did for all who are willing to look and see themselves, is to remove their blindness and enable them to see outwardly and inwardly, as he did for Bartimaeus and for the man born blind whose words echo the certainty of all such miracles of healing: "Whereas I was blind, now I see" *(John 9:25).* The gods of this world have blinded our minds and darkened our understanding and have alienated us from the life of God through the ignorance that is in them *(Ephesians 4:18; II Corinthians 4:4).*

The most important question of all for Christians is this: Where do we stand as we look and see Jesus Christ beside our own reflection in the mirror? Are we like blind men begging by a Jericho road or like children of God raised up with eyes open, moving along with him? Probably no one is ever completely in either category, but always somewhere in between. Begin wherever you are to pursue the shadowy figure of self which can lead to the point of recognition that all are a part of his creation and can be vehicles of his grace; that all can be open to the beauty and wonder of life, partaking deeply of the meaning of love in relationship, finding new meaning in the command to love him with all our minds; and that all of us can find in the world, terrible as it is, some of the goodness God has placed here for us to catch, to hold, and to fulfill.

If we go along with the cured-blindness approach to life, the closing words of the Jericho blind man's story will become our goal: "Receive thy sight: thy faith hath saved thee. And immediately he received his sight, and followed him, glorifying God" *(Luke 18:42-43)*.

Such a Lenten discipline means windows opening for us to see through, enabling us to sing a new song of thankfulness loud and long, as blindness, suddenly or gradually, gives way to sight. As our minds are cleared by this we are blind no longer to God's purpose for our lives.

O God, keep us from misleading thoughts and anxieties. Lead us into whatever is best for thee and for us; give us understanding sympathy and a full measure of common sense, that we may live this day more closely to thy plan for us; and keep us humble and loving above all things.

Third Week of Lent

III LENT

The Hidden Heart

PETER, or whoever wrote his epistle, speaks a phrase which describes the "heart" area of Lenten self-examination, "the hidden man of the heart" *(I Peter 3:4)*. Peter is speaking of "the inner man" where both good and evil lie—often hidden from view, but there.

That is why whenever we prepare for the Service of Holy Communion we pray first of all for God to "cleanse the thoughts of our hearts," thereby acknowledging humbly that all hearts are open to him, that he knows all human desires, and that from him no secrets are hid. Take a look, then, at the hidden man of *your* heart.

To the skilled doctor and surgeon there are few secrets left in the human heart on the physiological side, for they have stethoscoped, cardiographed, and opened up a great many of them.

But the secrets still hidden in that seat of our feelings and emotions, which is called the "heart," are legion. The secrets locked tightly within the human heart would make an unforgettable saga of heroism, sacrifice, and patient suffering, or an equally unforgettable saga of human degradation and demonic possession, or most often a mixture of the two. Such sagas would stir the hardest human heart to praise on the one hand, or to revulsion on the other.

The clergy come across these secrets in pastoral visits, in the confessional, in conferences with people, and in reading secular and religious books, papers, and magazines. They find, almost daily, examples of the unsung heroes of the human heart and those whose hearts are corroded by evil, all of them showing that "as a man thinketh in his heart, so is he" *(Proverbs 23:7)*. That is why we pray "cleanse the *thoughts* of our hearts."

The flow of the heart's blood to the brain makes it possible for us to think and to keep our senses alert. The heart, then, is a symbol of our inner life and holds the secrets of what we are and all the motivations for our conduct, good or bad. Therefore, everyone of us must know "the hidden man of the heart" before we can deal with it. The heart must be probed and its depths plumbed in order to find what is really there beneath the superficial appearances and the unheard thump of its beat. This week we will be doing this.

O Lord, forgive us if we have offended another, and let us know the offence and the one offended so that we may ask pardon and do what we can to make it up. Keep our relationships thoughtful and considerate, being ever sensitive to the needs of others and ready at all times to go the second mile in word or deed.

THIRD MONDAY

Delicate Probing

THE heart can be probed in several ways. For example, the hidden man of the heart stands naked before the psychiatrist, and often this is an essential therapy. Again, one's heart is stripped of all pretense in the presence of a priest, through confession; and this, too, is often required for the soul's health. Or, best of all, perhaps, for revealing the truth, a man comes to himself alone in the presence of God, opening his heart, baring its secrets, with no intermediary.

David E. Roberts began a sermon on "Christian Certainty" with these words: "Let us start, then, with man, no matter how much such a proposal may horrify some theologians." Paul Tillich, the well-known theologian, was not horrified at this statement, for he wrote the Introduction to *The Grandeur and Misery of Man,* in which this sermon is found. Dr. Tillich commented thus on the phrase: "The way to certainty is not through argument but through the courage to look at ourselves and to see ourselves as we really are, or, in other words, as we are in the eyes of the eternal which cannot be deceived by us."

One of the most shocking crimes and trials of the twentieth century, containing fantastic deceptions hidden in the human heart, was the famous Loeb-Leopold case in Chicago in the mixed up twenties, when two brilliant boys from respectable families committed a brutal murder simply for the excitement of it and to prove they were in the direct line of Nietzsche's Superman. The story of the hidden "thoughts of the heart" which revealed the source of this weird *Compulsion* was retold some years ago for all to read and ponder again.

Our attitudes and feelings, the thoughts of our hearts, play important roles, for they determine the course of our lives; and the man of the hidden heart, be he hero or heel, must reveal himself to himself and be judged by God at last for what he really is.

A prayer petition dropped into an intercession box in a parish church read, "I ask God for a miracle." We are constantly asking God for miracles without clearing the way for them to happen, without freeing our thoughts from the chains of self-deceit.

We ask for things without thinking of the consequences or what must be revealed in order to obtain them. We try to brush off the past, for example, as a speck of soot, but it won't brush off, so we try to shrug it off. Stock-taking often reveals a sad state, with the inside of the heart and mind looking like a long neglected store window, with all its dirt-laden merchandise.

This intimate look at self in the presence of Christ brings to mind Kierkegaard's famous description of what Lent should do to men. He said Lent should "strip men of their disguises, compel them to see evasions for what they are, label blind alleys, cut off men's retreats, tear down the niggardly roofs they continue to build over their precious sun dials, isolate men from the crowd, enforce self-examination; and bring them solitary and alone before the Eternal."

It is at one of these points that something usually happens to us and we turn to God, for cleansing first, then for refilling both mind and heart with a better grade of content.

It is most important that we feed the head and the heart with nourishing food. Remember how the seed, which is the Word of God, falls on good ground, lands in an honest heart, and grows, bringing forth abundant fruit with patience? That is, when it is heard, kept, and acted on, when our minds and hearts take it in. What "seed" is being sown to grow within your heart and mind? You had better look and see.

Take a more critical look, for example, at what you read, for your mind, heart, and life will be influenced by it. It is not a question of censorship, but of discrimination. Having seen and known the worst about life (and few have escaped this) why should men wallow in it? "Brethren, the time is short" *(I Corinthians 7:29)*. I bid you earnestly redeem it by what you read.

Dear Father, keep our minds free from involvement in the quirks and distortions of thought and in the futility of doubt and regret; save the best and the worst of us for responding to thy daily call of living life to the full; and please, dear God, keep our sense of humor in working order.

THIRD TUESDAY

The Inner Man

THE Christian Gospel is exemplified in the story of the Prodigal Son, which is the story of "the hidden heart." Feed for a moment on the content of this classic story of "man's need and God's action," Reuel Howe's wonderful phrase, which applies to all, involving the basic ideas of repentance, confession, and forgiveness. Even if one has never left home, the problem is the same. It can be that we are eating husks in the pigpens of a city far from home, or that we are chewing the cud of jealousy or uncharitableness or envy while staying right where we are. It is quite possible to be "at home," but not really at home in the sense of dwelling within the Father's presence. This applies to the Elder Brother even more, perhaps, than to the Prodigal Son.

Our inner self is the problem. Once we have had an open and honest look at ourselves, what can we do? Despair is the natural result. But God did not leave the highest of his creation to sink at last into such a morass. The Gospel, which Christians hold to be God's truth, is just this: that when we come to ourselves and have sense enough to go to our Father and ask his forgiveness (as the Prodigal Son did, and the Elder Brother did not), we find that we are accepted as we are and that God's love cleanses, heals, and restores.

The ability to look inward is a form of humility and the beginning of one's way back from whatever "far country" we are in. In Lent it is good to check the progress of the journey to see how close to home one is.

Lent is going fast. During the weeks that remain we all must work hard to complete the picture of ourselves. No better time will ever come than this season which is ready-made for the outsiders, those who are blind to our real selves and who often live in a world without meaningful values, to come to ourselves. There is sufficient time to seek to become insiders with spiritual sight restored, who feel wanted and who fit, for the first time, perhaps, into a normal framework of life, with at least some evidences of maturity and magnanimity, relatedness, and consciousness of the needs of others. Seize now your opportunity to discover "the hidden man of the heart" who is within you.

O God, help us this day, to keep calm in spite of stress, remembering that fret can spoil the day and that stewing over "fate" is foreign to thy will for us; keep us close to thy way of loving concern in all our relationships, and never let us fail to seek the best way and to avoid every lesser way, and to live our life to the utmost.

THIRD WEDNESDAY

Repent Ye

A VISIT to Holy Island calls for certain disciplines, four of which have already been mentioned—fasting, prayer, worship, and self-examination. But penitence is another important discipline necessary for the health of our inner life. Penitence means being sorry for our sins. But repentance is a stronger word and means an awareness of one's short-comings leading to a changed heart and amendment of life. When we are stung painfully enough by conscience over our sinfulness, penance of some kind is performed to show the depths of sorrow and repentance, eventuating in reconciliation with the person or persons sinned against, and restoration to the full life of the Christian fellowship.

This does not refer, however, to the severe penance and extreme self-mortification of a St. Cuthbert, who lived as a hermit on one of the lonely Farnes, but points to the path of penitence Joel urged on those who had strayed from God's way and were firmly held in the grip of worshiping false gods and false goals. "Turn ye even to me, saith the Lord, . . . and rend your heart, and not your garments" *(Joel 2:12-13)*.

Just as Joel called the people back from their ways to God's way and pleaded with them to slip out from under the heathen yoke, so did those saints on Holy Island alternate between monkish apartness and missionary zeal, sallying forth from their island cloister to convert the northern parts of Britain. Just as Jesus admonished the first disciples to proclaim "repentance and remission of sins" *(Luke 24:47)*, so did the saints who peopled Holy Island preach in his name. Just as John Baptist preached in the wilderness, and Jesus began his ministry with the message of "the baptism of repentance for the remission of sins" *(Mark 1:4)*, so the saints obeyed the command "repent ye, and believe the gospel" *(Mark 1:15)*, which are recorded as the first and last words Jesus gave to his disciples on earth.

Of course the word "disciple" comes from the same root as discipline. A disciple is a pupil, a willing learner. Therefore, for the Christian disciple, discipline means guidance under Christ as teacher, who helps us to have attitudes and to follow behavior more commensurate with the Christian faith.

The discipline of penitence involves consciousness of sin and sorrow for it, restitution as far as possible, and accepting God's forgiveness while at the same time forgiving oneself and others. The best good news of the Gospel is the promise of a gracious welcome to all penitent sinners from a merciful God.

Any visit to Holy Island, then, calls the pilgrim to fit the key of repentance to the lock of his or her own heart and open it up to God. This penitence means a personal response to the inner awareness of one's need, leading to some definite penance as an outward manifestation of sorrow and evidence of the sincerity of one's response to his call, "Repent ye."

Lent, as a Holy Island, is reminiscent of Christ's forty days in the wilderness fighting against earthly temptations. As a start in becoming *penitent* sinners, review for a moment his several temptations and check them against our yieldings to temptations. He was tempted by the Devil to attract attention by a few spectacular miracles, such as turning stone to bread, making a giant leap defying gravity, and becoming a world conqueror and dictator. He was tempted by the hope of realizing the Kingdom of God on earth without delay. He refused to yield, for in each case what the Devil urged was contrary to God's will. We are tempted by status, by worldly values, by expediency in the face of criticism, by non-involvement and non-understanding of the needs of others. We do not live by bread alone. We must take God on faith. We must worship only God. Immediately after the temptations in the wilderness, Jesus began to preach, calling on the people for a change of heart. After his experience of fasting in the wilderness, the Devil let him be, and he was hungry. God came and ministered to his wants *(Matthew 4:1-11)*.

The disciplines on Holy Island whet our appetites for that which feeds our souls, leading us to take on a new diet for our recently cleansed spiritual life.

Come swiftly, O Lord, to the dark moments when we are lost. Make us aware of thy presence. Strengthen us to

67

resist the urges and pulls to deeper darkness. Stir us to move away from the dark moments of sinfulness toward the light of thy forgiveness. Come quickly, O Lord, as we call—or forget to call—and keep thou close to us and keep us close to thee this day and night, and as far as the days and nights stretch before us.

THIRD THURSDAY

Mortification

ASHES on the first day of Lent may have been heaped upon one's soul figuratively to acknowledge the need for repentance. But only in this sense should Christians be sad and mourn. The Christian life begins with repentance, "We have erred, and strayed . . . like lost sheep," but goes on to alleluia, forgiveness, and belonging. It is worth wading through the shallows of misery in order to enter into the deeps of lasting joy. By God's help the interior life approaches repentance in the spirit of conquering, of making a victorious onslaught against any down-sittings, backslidings, or acceptances of defeat.

Probably the hardest lesson for us to learn is that there must be repentance, a turning away from the old life, before a new way of life can begin. When the old life is purged away, through confession and surrender to God's will as completely as possible, newness of life begins to emerge. The absolution speaks of "all those who with hearty repentance and true faith turn unto him." Repentance, then, enables us to be emptied of all blocks, frustrations, and sins, so that something better can be poured in. For there must be riddance of the bad or very little good can be added to the already filled-up receptacle of self. What we push out as not wanted must be replaced by something we want which ministers to our soul's health.

Antique experts have long since developed eyes to see and recognize fine furniture hidden under several layers of thick paint. By patience and hard work they remove the paint and restore the piece. The scars and wear of the years are revealed, but the original stands as it was first made, and once again fills its intended place.

Penitence is the paint remover, and our Holy Island is the place and time for applying it, allowing it to do its work, then scraping off the softened layers of sinful pride, selfish living, over-indulgence, and "phony" fronts, which have obscured the real self. We were made to live by the power of God and, while the original sin of selfishness obtrudes and the choice between darkness and light is always before us, we are restless and unsatisfied until we find restoration and oneness with the God who made us, until Christ is actually alive and made manifest in us.

The Christian religion is clear in its demands for penitence. Having done with life on the shallow level of self-centeredness, the penitent sinner gives forth at last with certainty the cry which has been stifled all along, "O Lord, *my* God."

The word "mortification" often conveys the impression of practicing such extreme physical disciplines as flagellations, wearing hair shirts, and keeping lengthy vigils, as if it were connected with a "dark night of the soul" experience; it is also thought to be something reserved for saints who seem to enjoy and benefit from such things. But the meaning is far simpler and much more satisfying.

69

Mortification means growth, change, development, dying to sin and rising to new life. Paul uses the term "transformed" in at least two places: "Be ye transformed by the renewing of your mind" *(Romans 12:2)* and "Transforming themselves into the apostles of Christ" *(II Corinthians 11:13).*

The Christian goes ahead on the basic assumption that sinful human nature can be changed. The seed or bulb planted or buried in the earth brings forth new life and it is transformed by dying and becomes a new creation. But the life is really not new at all, for the new life is showing forth that which was potentially present all the time. Something similar happens when one dies to self-centeredness and rises to a new concern for persons and things beyond self. This is all part of the total transformation, the dying to self-centered babyhood and rising to an other-centered and mature adulthood.

Curbing self is part of the discipline of mortification. When we grow in Christ we come under the yoke of Christ and he begins to tell us what to do. Self is no longer dictator. Christ leads us and we follow him. He transforms the common round, the trivial task. He makes every morning new. He works through the efforts we make to follow his prompting. He enables us to accept our little crosses patiently and generously by the power and grace of his Holy Spirit.

Repentance is the step all of us must take if life is to be lived on a different basis and if we are to demonstrate by the new way we live—unselfishly, by love—that penance (which partakes of the nature of a sacrament) has become a part of our daily life.

Radiance shines through most of the characters in the

New Testament and those who made Lindisfarne "holy," for their practice of the discipline of penance was positive, not negative. There is no morbidity recorded of true saints. They possess an imperishable sense of humor which is God-given. They have the immense capacity to stand apart objectively and to laugh at themselves. There is no "cheap melancholy" here but an intense love of life and whatever ministers to its growth.

Dear Lord and Father of us all, we thank thee for the days of our years which have been lived and are yet to be lived. Help us to be worthy of thy blessings. Keep us on the alert for opportunities to show forth thy love so that our tongues may be guarded from speaking hurtful words and our faces from looks which may be misunderstood. May we rejoice in the life given this day and live it according to thy will.

THIRD FRIDAY

Peter's Penitence

An illustration of repentance is the story of Peter's sin and Peter's penitence *(Matthew 26:69-75)*. Peter's sin of the denial of Christ is common to all and need not be dwelt on. But the great lesson of Peter's penitence also concerns all, and his final act of return is full of the deepest spiritual meaning, beyond a cock crow and a stinging moment of betrayal.

Peter heard, in the midst of being afraid and ashamed to own Christ, the accusing query, "Peter, where [who] is your God?" It was only when penitence drove him to his

71

knees that he could cry again, "O Lord, my God."

Peter's experience is like walking down a long road through desert land, away from the mountains, the heights, the greenness, toward barrenness and darkness. Then, as the dullness, dustiness, and strain slow the walker's movements, he begins to wonder about the terrain and the destination and suddenly realizes he is off course.

When this moment comes to any of us we are ready for a sudden tap on the shoulder from behind, or a voice calling our name; and when the tap is felt or the voice is heard, we stop, turn, and see for the first time what we have been walking away from.

Any wise person, when they realize they are wandering aimlessly on their own, lost, turns around and begins walking away from the desert land and its lifeless plain, back toward the mountains; and the psalmist's cry becomes their cry, "I will lift up mine eyes unto the hills, from whence cometh my help" *(Psalm 121:1).*

Holy Island is a time and a place for penitence as well as for fasting, prayer, worship, and self-appraisal; it is a period of traveling back toward oneness with the God whom, unrepentant, we often fail.

Judas went out and in his loneliness and despair hanged himself, for he had never really *heard* his Master's teachings on forgiveness. Peter went out, repented in deep sorrow, and found his way back to God by accepting his forgiveness, because God had accepted his penitence. There was no time lag, no procrastination to slow his penitence. Peter allowed no time for his sin and guilt feelings to grow, once he discovered them, but did what he knew had to be done without delay. And for Peter the chains were broken; for him the time of alleluia had come. We often put off repenting, hoping a less costly way can be found. *But there is no easier way.*

Confession, forgiveness, and restoration are Christ's answers to such denials as Peter's. The purpose of any visit to Holy Island is to bring about repentance, whereby we forsake sin. When that moment of turning comes, when that prickle of realization on the back of one's neck is felt, God is near; when defeat and frustration break down pride, when we come to any moment and know our strength is not sufficient, when we, as we must at last, come to ourselves in the presence of God, then we dare not delay the journey from the wastelands of our own way, back to the triumphant life which is God's way.

Good Lord, keep the devastation in the world from devastating our hearts. Keep the cruelty of man to man from warping our minds. By thy grace prevent us from allowing bitterness to destroy our souls, resentment to shut up our compassion, and suffering to shatter our faith. Keep us, Good Lord, from living in the irreparable past by yielding it to thee, and let us live only in the forgiven and forgiving present, with hearts full of thanks and with minds full of hope and trust, based on the blessed knowledge that nothing can separate us from thee to whom the future ultimately belongs.

THIRD SATURDAY

Words and the Word

THE Lindisfarne Gospels were written and illuminated by two bishops about A.D. 724. Tradition says the manuscript was washed overboard in a storm while Bishop Eardulf was taking it to Ireland for safekeeping before a Danish invasion in 875, and that it floated back to safety at low tide and was recovered. The Gospels have been reproduced by a Swiss firm. This costly and limited edition has turned out to be surprisingly in demand, with its color photographs of the original manuscript which has resided in the British Museum since 1753.

The book which Eadfrith wrote, which Ethilwald impressed on the outside and carved "as well as he knew how to do," which Billfrith, the Anchorite, adorned, and which Aldred, "unworthy and most miserable priest," glossed for God and St. Cuthbert, is a treasure all should see when they visit London.

The manuscript is composed of 258 leaves of stout vellum, each page 13½ x 9¾ inches, in a remarkable state of preservation. The manuscript contains the four Gospels, St. Jerome's Epistle to Damascus, and the Eusebian Canon, all in Latin. At the end is a note in English giving the traditional origin; and there is an interlinear English word-for-word translation. The illuminations were copies from Byzantine and South Italian originals, and the pages were decorated with interlaced creatures and strap-work (a narrow fillet or band folded, crossed, and sometimes interlaced) in magnificent Northumbrian style.

The monks on Holy Island preserved the precious Word by copying painfully with scratchy quills the life- and light-giving words. The light which shone from the book penetrated the darkness and guided their way through ignorance, danger, temptation, and trial.

Holy Island stands for the great theme of the Bible as found in St. John's Gospel: "The light is still shining in the darkness, for the darkness has never put it out" *(John 1:5, Goodspeed's Translation)*.

The Word and the Sacraments are the stabilizing ele- ments on Holy Island. They must be used together as the two stimuli for living the devotional life. We must keep in touch with the fountain and source—God's Word in his Book—and it must sustain and direct us in our post-Holy- Island life.

Halford E. Luccock tells this story of his youth. Hal and a few of his rebellious young friends decided to do the most wicked thing they could think of—burn the Bible. They took the huge book from his father's library and consigned it to the flames—a singularly common occur- rence in the history of religion. The senior Luccock arrived on the scene unexpectedly and immediately spoiled their fun by pointing out that the huge book was not the Bible at all but the dictionary, containing the same words, of course, but in a slightly different arrangement— and that they could not destroy words by burning, only by not using them.

The young Luccock, as he grew up and became a dis- tinguished professor at Yale University and very familiar with the Bible, would agree that burning the Book is not so wicked as ignoring it and that one can never be quite rid of it either by burning or by ignoring.

The Bible is not for burning, for it is the promised way out of darkness, and if its words are to have special significance for those who sit in darkness they cannot burn it or ignore it, but must examine it with care.

Save us from resentment this day, good Lord, and from that "poor me" feeling. As the day begins, lift us above the petty hurts which drag us down; lead us into the day's life forgiven and forgiving. Keep us conscious of thy presence all day long, so that any tendencies which arise within to make us feel resentful and hurt, may be put to rout by thoughts of thee. When the day ends, give us thankful hearts for all the blessings which have come our way.

Fourth Week of Lent

IV LENT

New Treasures

THE Bible did not really belong to the people and become a part of their lives until the invention of the printing press brought wide distribution in the vernacular and the Reformation gave them freedom to read it. In Green's *Short History of the English People* is this testimony: "No greater moral change ever passed over a nation than passed over England in the latter part of the reign of the first Queen Elizabeth. England became the people of a book, and that book was the Bible. Because of it, the whole moral tone of the nation was changed."

In the Elizabethan age the English language reached full flower; today most people acknowledge the King James version of the Bible to be the finest expression of that age. But the great Reformation heritage is that all people can read the Scriptures in their own tongue and find out for themselves what is there. Today it is possible to read the Bible in over a thousand tongues and in many excellent translations. In India this Reformation heritage is well guarded in the Service of Holy Communion in the Church of South India as the Bible is brought from the congregation at every service and presented to the officiating minister to read. The Bible belongs to the people who claim it. Today the Book is open for us to use as a guidebook on the Holy Island of Lent.

Since lanterns and flashlights are scarce in India, people often use a limb from the neem tree to light their pathway through the darkness. It burns slowly, like punk, but keeps a glow sufficiently bright to guide one's steps, provided the branch is waved back and forth gently to keep it burning. Similarly, those who read the Holy Scripture regularly find that it sheds enough light for each step they take.

Someone has truly said, "The world is not done with this Book, but the world is done for without it." "The word of our God shall stand for ever" *(Isaiah 40:8)*. "I know this book is the word of God," said an old Mohave Indian chief, "because it pulls my heart."

It does pull one's heart as well as clear one's mind; for as we receive the profound inner meaning of the ancient, yet timely stories, characters, and passages, they hit home as hard today as they did in the beginning, when men wrote down the words under the white heat of inspiration and conviction which stirred their souls. We still must live under the same basic law of God as did Moses, and suffer the same consequences of disobeying it; we still must reach beyond ourselves to God for wisdom and strength to handle life adequately, as did the prophets; we still will go unsatisfied unless we find faith and hope, like that found by the psalmists, to fill our fearful hearts.

The Word of God does not depend on literal inerrancy as held by our forefathers, or on the modern dress of new translations demanded in our day, but on God's truth as it comes to us who seek it in the context of our own existence.

"The Bible is a strange book to the modern man, not

mainly because of differences of language and symbol, but principally because it has a different view of human nature and human destiny. It speaks of the Divine initiative, of grace, of us as responsive to God's word. The Christian Gospel in the New Testament speaks to a condition and a need of which we are only fitfully aware. It demands a detachment for which we have little time. It confronts us with a drama of human destiny in which our favorite character part does not appear."*

Open, then, the Book and seek greater familiarity with the "whole counsel of God." Even in its most primitive parts "it is the record of those great spirits of our race who have been discovered of God."*

O God, ease the fears of our hearts while reading headlines and imagining possible actions beyond our knowing or control. Fill our minds instead with enough faith to continue living unafraid. Give us enough common sense to make the best of any moment in time, in the sure and certain hope that the world is thine and that whatever we do cannot at last thwart the coming of thy kingdom; through Christ, our Lord.

FOURTH MONDAY

Bible Stories and Characters

THERE are great stories which challenge us on almost every page of the Bible, which throw new light on how to live more nearly as God wants us to live, and these stories

*Roy McKay, from an address given when he was the head of religious broadcasting for the BBC, London, April, 1957.

yield new treasures each time they are read. Take two samples, one from the Old Testament and one from the New—the Call of Jeremiah *(1:4-10),* and the Prodigal Son *(Luke 15:11-32).* Jeremiah discovered that God is a personal God, approachable and accessible to all who call upon him. God removed the fear that kept Jeremiah from growing up, implanted a keen moral sense in him, and gave him spiritual insight that clarified judgment. Read this great story of Jeremiah's devotional life and learn how God kept close to this prophet all his days, and made him strong. The Lord said to Jeremiah, "Behold, I have put my words in thy mouth." The story of the Prodigal Son is found only in St. Luke's Gospel and it shows where man's rebellion and effort to escape from his Father must always end. "And when he came to himself . . . he arose, and came to his father."

There are many allegorical stories which never grow old, the deep meaning of which is needed by all of us— Adam and Eve, the inevitable consequences of disobedience and man's desire to get away from God, to be "as gods" and "know it all" *(Genesis 3:1-24);* Jacob at Bethel *(Genesis 28:16-22),* the discovery that God is in every place wherever we may go. There are parables, such as the story of the Good Samaritan *(Luke 10:25-37),* that one's neighbor is recognized in the person of everyman; we read of Nicodemus coming to Christ by night *(John 3:1-11),* the search for truth, when conscience will not be stilled.

But the most important record of all is that of God Incarnate in Jesus Christ and the meaning of his existence as God's revelation of himself to all. So read and learn from the great teachings of the Bible.

There are great characters, too, who make the stories

come to life as they stand on tiptoe showing the way for a many-sided approach to God and pointing out ways of responding to him in worship and acts. Take Moses *(Exodus 3:2-6)*, who led a nation to greatness, and Ananias *(Acts 9:10-22)*, who helped complete one man's conversion: both answered God's call to go for him.

When the lives of these men who were God's instruments in the world are read, we find that their greatness increased in direct ratio to their dependence upon and obedience to him. In many instances the response to God's call was reluctant. Moses tried hard to escape responsibility, claiming he was no speaker. But once he accepted what God placed on him, he led God's people to freedom and formulated God's law for all who would dwell together in peace and harmony.

Anyone can follow a plan of Bible reading, with a little discipline, during such a season as Lent, and find God saying something significant for all to hear. There are great passages galore; but to open up new paths in the deep waters we must read, ponder, and apply with persistence and regularity, reading as hungry disciples, passionately concerned with what God is trying to tell us through the words, the people, and the incidents.

Some phrases from such reading will stick for later recall: "Thou shalt be called, The repairer of the breach, The restorer of paths to dwell in" *(Isaiah 58:12);* "Entreat me not to leave thee" *(Ruth 1:16);* "I know that my redeemer liveth" *(Job 19:25);* "Come unto me . . . and I will give you rest" *(Matthew 11:28).* "I will put my law in their inward parts, and write it in their hearts" *(Jeremiah 31:33);* "The people that walked in darkness have seen a great light" *(Isaiah 9:2);* "The kingdom of God is within you" *(Luke 17:21);* "Ye shall receive power" *(Acts 1:8);* "But the greatest of these is charity [love]" *(I Corinthians 13:13).*

Many great passages scattered from Genesis to Revelation endure, as well as many stories and characters, for they give us glimpses of the Eternal.

Dear God, help us to find our way out of the past into thy way of forgiveness and love. Help us to be honest and to make the direction of our days conform to what we know of thee in Jesus Christ, our Lord, in whose name we pray and in whose way we would walk.

FOURTH TUESDAY

Making a Meditation

THE prophetic authority from the authentic Word of God comes from living so close to Jesus Christ that his way becomes *The Way* for us.

Lesslie Newbigin, a bishop in the Church of South India, in his fine book, *The Reunion of the Church,* has this to say about "authority":

"Jesus produced no 'authority' (although he spoke with authority). The authority with which he met men, with which he taught, with which he cast out devils, was in himself alone. It was the personal authority of Truth, for he is the Truth. It was the authority of God, the Creator of men, who has made men to recognize himself. The truth of the Gospel cannot be possessed apart from personal faith in the living Christ."

Our understanding of Christ's authority comes as we

82

deepen our understanding of the Bible, and comes only by intimate study and meditation.

Making a meditation means, as seen in Christ, simply fixing our minds on God and giving him our full attention, drawing near to God by thinking of him. It is only by looking at Jesus Christ that we are able to begin to understand what God is like. Did not Jesus say, "He that hath seen me hath seen the Father" *(John 14:9)?* If we want to be brought near to God and to find his presence a real and living thing, we must look at Jesus Christ as he is revealed in the four Gospels. Jesus is the Way, the Guide who leads us to the Father, and the Gospels give us a living picture of him who leads us into God's presence.

Great Christian living grows out of knowledge and understanding of the Bible. Anyone who is a Christian will study God's Word, and anyone who studies and meditates will find inspiration for witnessing to the truth that God has not left us in a hopeless dilemma, but has provided a way to pass through the mountainous impasse of sin and ignorance. God's love was expended all the way to enable us to do this. God has acted to show all of us his way and to save us from our own ways.

"Most of us have had the experience of visiting some great museum in which we have strolled around looking wonderingly at its vast store of varied and interesting treasures, and yet feeling rather lost, wishing that we had an expert guide who could explain to us what it all meant."* Commentaries and devotional manuals attempt to do just this. Take the time to ask and answer three

*Alan Richardson, *A Preface to Bible Study,* Westminster, Philadelphia, 1944, pp. 8-9.

questions concerning the passage read: What does it mean? What does it mean to me? What must I do about it?

"The Bible is the only source of first-hand witness concerning the Person through whom God revealed the saving knowledge of himself to the World, and it is in the pages of this Book that the personal encounter with the Person of Christ takes place" *(Alan Richardson).*

Since the Lectionary in *The Book of Common Prayer* is extensive and complete and much too much to be read daily with full appreciation, a selection, or miniature lectionary, might prove a more helpful daily reading guide for the beginner. The second lessons at Evening Prayer for the Sundays and weekdays of Lent, for example. Or take the Lenten *Forward Day by Day* and read the passage of Scripture suggested for each day. Once begun and fitted firmly into one's daily routine, the habit is easily continued.

Dear Lord, open our hearts and minds to a new under-standing of thy Word; give us courage and calmness and confidence for facing whatever lies ahead this day; and keep us in the straight and sure way of thy peace, through Jesus Christ.

FOURTH WEDNESDAY

Read, Mark, and Learn

A few simple admonishments and encouragements:
Read the Bible because you are a Christian; because you hunger and thirst for a life worth living; because you wish to know the history of religion; because in this Book

God the Creator speaks his living Word to you and unfolds his purpose of salvation in Jesus Christ.*

Live by the Bible, although there are many parts of the Bible you may not understand at first reading. But there are many parts of the Bible you *do* understand, which point the way for you to walk; these words throw light on your path.

Use the Lectionary placed in back of the Prayer Book to suggest content and continuity in Bible reading; it goes hand in hand with prayer and the other disciplines of the devotional life.

Use the Prayer Book, since a large portion of *The Book of Common Prayer* is taken from the Bible and keeps all who use it close to the Word of God.

Try reading a modern translation. Several new translations of the New Testament are very good—Goodspeed, Moffatt, Knox, Rieu, the Revised Standard Version, Phillips, and The New English Bible. *The Short Bible* for the Old and New Testaments is particularly helpful, because it gives an introduction to each book.

Read devotional classics and other devotional books which appear each year and nourish your devotional life.

Any person can retire to one of the hidden rocks and caves on Holy Island, in imagination, like those holy men of Lindisfarne really did, for a quiet time with God's Holy Word and for stirring up the inner fire. Those who do so return with joy to the mainland ready to take up the opportunities for service and witness which come their way. Indeed we must use such a regular discipline before any rewarding understanding comes.

---

*Indebted to Suzanne de Dietrich for these suggestions, from *Discovering the Bible,* World Council of Churches, N.Y., pp. 1-2.

Every night the lamps are burning in front of the Church of the Ascension on Fifth Avenue in the city of New York, beckoning those who pass to stop, turn aside, enter, and pray. These twin gleams in the dark hold the promises of inner light which warms and dispels the cold mists of life. So God's Word gives light to those who walk in darkness. From the Word of God comes a powerful sense of his presence. From it we gain a glimpse of humility shaming our arrogance, a demonstration of industry highlighting our sloth, a note of courage piercing our cowardice, an awakening to some incident in our narrow-gauge living which is racing toward a collision with a situation which we cannot dodge or handle alone. God is ever near to us in Christ.

Lent tells us not that he is in a Book or in a promise, but that he is in a Life, and that in that Life is our redemption, when that Life is accepted into our life. Lent reminds us of "the sobering aspects of judgment, sudden and irrevocable, the shutting of a door, the springing of a trap" when we chose to ignore God. But Lent also tells us, in the parable of the fig tree in leaf, for example, that out of death can come life, out of distress can come redemption, and out of evil can come good.

"The Bible shows life in process, reaching on from that which is primitive and partial to that which shall be complete in him; and the long procession of its human figures culminates in the measure of the stature of the fulness of Christ" *(Suzanne de Dietrich).*

In the Book is God's truth for every age. Burn it, or damn it, but do not ignore it, for in it is the straight Word of God the Creator to restore and redeem your life and enrich it abundantly. You are the people of the Book which changes men and nations. Hear, then, and hearken unto it.

Dear Lord, make manifest through us this day some measure of thy love. Help us to open blind eyes to the wonders of thy life. Put us up against forces so strong we must constantly seek thy strength. Use us as thy messengers to those who have not listened to nor heard thee. Put a trumpet in our hands with the will and the wind to blow it for thee; in Christ's name we ask.

FOURTH THURSDAY

Resentment's Cure

FOR special services held on Holy Island during the year, worshipers stream across at low tide when the water recedes for a few hours and the island becomes a part of the mainland. A line of twenty-foot poles marks the route through a crossing of the stream Lindis at "The Low," and this trail is called "The Pilgrim's Way." With the well-barnacled poles set at rakish angles on one side, and the centuries-old cairns (rock piles) laid by the monks to guide the pilgrims of long ago from the mainland on the other side, the way is easily traversed in safety, afoot or by vehicle. Just in case the quick-running tide rushes in too fast or a visitor does not start in time to make the crossing to or from, two refuge shelters stand on spindly legs to rescue them. "Theet's for seeving leef," as the natives describe them. Today the fast-moving taxis skirt the Snook and hug the shore to escape the incoming tide as long as possible.

While very few lives have been lost, either in shifting quicksands or through lack of judgment and ignorance of the tides, only the clearly marked passage and the careful charting of the tides have prevented many from perishing. This holds true for our life's journey, God's word charting the way.

Have you ever battered against a stone wall and found it literally breaking you to pieces, while at the same time you cannot make a single crack in the wall? There are many kinds of walls against which we hurl ourselves in futility. Some we erect ourselves and use as excuses for our attitudes or conduct. Some walls we cannot break down, for they define our own limitations. But there are a few walls which bring us up short to remind us of God's way of dealing with situations, and we see that his way is better than our own battering-ram technique.

In Isaiah are these words: "But thou shalt call [those] walls [thy] Salvation" *(60:18),* for they yield to God's way as if by magic, and as we approach them under his guidance they disappear. After such an experience we can say with Paul, "and [he] hath broken down the middle wall of partition between us" *(Ephesians 2:14).*

The wall of personal resentment blocks off many from God and everyone else. The sense of being wronged by another, and the erection of a wall which separates, isolates us and brings a seething misery which eats at our inner peace. Resentment always does the greatest harm to the one who carries the galling, poisonous burden of it.

God was in Christ reconciling the world to himself. Christ is in all reconciling them unto himself and to each other. His reconciling Spirit is the opposite of self-centeredness. This wall of tangled evil and ill-will, by which we are separated, dissolves like the walls of an Indian mud hut in the monsoon floods, when the spirit of forgiveness replaces resentment. This is true no matter what the cause of it may be, even though one feels the person or word or incident or wrongdoing has spoiled his life forever. When we offend others, and they erect a wall of resentment against us and the world, there is only one Christian solution—forgiveness. Jesus gave his life to teach us this great redemptive fact which he exemplified in all he taught and did. We deny him as Lord when we fail to follow his lead and remain resentful and unforgiving, often without the other person ever knowing why.

No matter how wrong the other has been, no matter how much harm they have done, no matter whether they repent or not, when the offended one has forgiven, the burden drops, the wall tumbles down, and the chances for the other's redemption have increased a thousandfold. Those who won't forgive, always waiting for the other to make the first move, cannot enter into the experience of being forgiven themselves. The Lord's Prayer makes this perfectly clear: "Forgive us our trespasses, as we forgive those who trespass against us." This is the only condition in the entire prayer. Forgiveness is to enter into and "to share in the redeeming work of Christ."

Each time a church service is attended, we are reminded of the barriers which will surely shatter us unless we allow God to reverse our walking or thinking or speaking. Any trip to Holy Island provides time and opportunity for breaking the deadlock of resentment and opening up the penitential, Christlike way of forgiveness.

Resentment is a common problem which spoils life and can threaten its destruction, moving as quickly as the tides of the North Sea swirling in to isolate Holy Island. Deal with it swiftly.

O God, help us examine our motives and make us honestly face what we see. Let no unworthy intention remain, but clear our minds of selfishness. In our thoughts and in our desires keep our minds centered on thee and thy will, and keep us humble.

FOURTH FRIDAY

Breaking the Barrier

MAN has at last broken through the sound barrier by flying an airplane faster than sound. Until then it was thought that at the speed of sound there was a mysterious unbreakable wall which we could not crash through. The dramatic moment of breaking through the sound barrier came at last after stubborn, courageous, and tragic attempts, with the discovery that beyond the speed of sound the controls of the plane must be reversed to avoid disaster. When the controls are reversed, the sound barrier is no longer a cosmic wall against which we must forever dash ourselves to pieces. At the point of apparently inevitable destruction, the pilot reverses the controls and continues uninterruptedly on the flight pattern in safety.

A major concern of Christ's ministry was to show us that if we attempt to control our own lives, our own destiny, with self as our only concern, we shall dash into a stone wall which will never yield. But if we reverse the controls, turn to God and let him handle our lives, and follow his way, the middle wall of partition will be broken down. Any wall which brings us up short and makes us realize that our way is not his way can be our salvation.

An excellent example of resentment's cure came one day in a letter a rector received from one of his former parishioners. She had been serving her parish as a volunteer director of religious education for a long time. Through the years she had been studying, going to conferences, and really applying herself to learn more about that field. Recently she wrote and told her former rector she had applied for the job of Director of Religious Education in her present parish. The rector there gave her many reasons why he could not consider her for the position. He talked to her honestly and frankly, reminding her to watch out for her seeming need for the "limelight," her need for praise, and a few other personal traits which he felt were stumbling blocks to others. In the end, he refused her the job. At first she felt shattered because she really had a deep sense of commitment to her work and a desire to serve the Church in this capacity. She wrote her old rector the whole story. He realized that whatever he said must be encouraging, and yet must hold her up and stretch her. So he wrote a long reply immediately, but felt it wasn't adequate and didn't mail it for over a week. Then he re-read it, added some thoughts in longhand, and sent it off, praying it would help.

Then a second letter came from her containing what follows, which she is willing to share with you. Her letter is a case history of how one person, by God's help, dealt with resentment and how her middle wall of partition was broken down and became her salvation. Here is her letter:

Someone wrote that "by a sublime paradox the fruits of denial are infinitely sweeter than the fruits of desire"—and I've never agreed with that or appreciated the real meaning until lately with the denial of that D.R.E.-ship. It now appalls me that I could possibly have wanted it so badly that I reacted in the manner I did—like a child not getting her way—fighting, biting and scratching, and running to you with the whole story. Certainly the Lord in his infinite wisdom let you cogitate what to write while the child did a bit of growing up—for your prayers (and mine) must have been answered as I "simmered" down and in the process acquired a bit of dignity I might have needed. Much as I would have put the rector out of my mind, that one "corny" phrase of his stuck—"Let go, let God!" So I did, and it isn't corny nor just a catch phrase, but humility itself. It was a bitter pill to swallow to return to church the following Sunday. I think I started to use the phrase then, and I prayed I wouldn't let resentment get the best of me and that no church job could stand in the way of my faith, and it worked. I resolved that if I had to peel potatoes for a church dinner, or sew for those in need, that I'd do it to the glory of God. And oddly enough I caught a glimmer of peace I haven't known before, of doing something nobody's going to praise me for—of doing something anyone else could do, but with a special sort of feel about it. I hope you gather what I'm rambling on about. Somehow it just doesn't matter much any more. The resentment, the hurt pride, slipped away as though it had never been there. I even attended a church school faculty meeting last week (I had vowed to myself I wouldn't) and was pleasant and normal and tried to apply that word empathy in which the rector said I was so lacking.

I had thought, too, of taking a "sabbatical leave,"

but have been doing just what comes to hand—my library work, rehearsing the Cherub choir, and any other odd job. . . .

Thank you for your letter. I'm glad now that you didn't mail it at once for I feel that I really have come a long way in a few weeks and maybe needed to get slapped down to stand more erectly. A lot of things the rector said are true—we just hate hearing the truth about ourselves, I suppose. In his own way, though, he has, as you said, courage and honesty to his credit, and has probably aided me spiritually whether I liked it or not.

The former rector still hears from this person and she still has her sense of joy over "resentment's cure," but she can never rest on her oars. The temptation to resent is always ready to strike when we relax and lay aside our weapons of prayer and humility.

Good Lord of our life, we need thee, for we are not sure of the way we should go this day. Many ways call our feet, but we can walk only one of them. We do not mind hardship or danger or even suffering if there is a chance to serve thee. We want to be useful. We want our life to count. So we come to thee asking which way we must take for thee today.

FOURTH SATURDAY

Antipathy

THE life-spoiling condition of antipathy is another version of resentment which must be mentioned as a variation on the same theme.

Antipathy is a form of antagonism of one human being toward another. Antipathy means incompatibility and is opposed to sympathy. It ranges in intensity from dislike to loathing. It can be caused by any number of things, but adds up to a broken relationship, something to be mended, or a wall of separation which must come down. Some people are naturally likeable and others are drawn to them. Some are instinctively disliked, many times for no real reason. The greatest labor of Christians must be for the disliked ones.

In that striking book, *The Nun's Story,* the discipline of relationship is ever to the fore in the "Living Rule of the Order." Sister Luke, whose story it is, learned many hard lessons in how to get along with the other Sisters. One lesson which stood her in good stead was this: "For those whom we instinctively dislike, try to do something. Remember ... the golden rule for antipathy is to ask to do a service for the one your spirit withdraws from."

That is a good answer for this soul-harming feeling toward another. It is the second-mile approach and conforms to Jesus' words: ". . . for if ye love them which love you, what reward have ye? do not even the publicans the same? And if ye salute your brethren only, what do ye necessary thereafter, to overcome this dangerous feeling more than others? do not even the publicans so?" *(Matthew 5:46-47)*.

It is true that some people just naturally rub us the wrong way, and it follows that there are those whom we affect the same. The Christian strives, by God's help, to correct within whatever is a stumbling block to another, and then to take the first step, and as many steps as may be of antagonism toward another. To let the condition remain untouched is to invite spiritual disaster. If a known state of antipathy exists, ask for direction as to what God wants you to do, and do it without delay "that ye may be the children of your Father" *(Matthew 5:45)*. When this "golden rule" is applied, the results are amazing—relationships are mended, walls are removed.

An old hymn adds a pertinent postscript of two lines to those who bear resentments and hold antipathies: *If our love were but more simple, We should take him at his word.*

For the God who created all mankind sent his Son to show that love and forgiveness are better than hate and resentment. But we are a stubborn lot, so often as "Christians" refusing to react as Christians, and thus preventing ourselves from growing out of the milk-and-sugar stage of religion and becoming grown-up sons and daughters of the Father. "Many be called, but few chosen" *(Matthew 20:6)*—but the few who are helped to find a way to cure resentment and antipathy make the ministry of all believers a glorious task. One can see people growing spiritually, just as one can see children growing taller. And the wonderful thing is, there is no end to it—to children's height, yes, but not to one's spiritual stature. New insight and understanding wait for all who stand under God's judgment and who accept his illuminating love which breaks down the wall of partition between us. But there are those who refuse to grow, who get bogged down in the mire of resentment, refusing to learn that any present moment can be a time of change for us, so that even this wall can be our salvation.

Jesus is still asking us to reverse the controls, to yield to his control if we have not already done so. If we are aware of what we are and if resentment or antipathy is present as a wall against which we dash ourselves in vain, may we, by his grace, forgive and be forgiven, so that the flight of our lives shall no longer be shattered at either barrier. It may be the most difficult thing we have ever done, but it is the only way to break through resentment and find inner peace and to open the way to reconciliation.

Isaiah gave a clue: "But thou shalt call [those] walls [thy] Salvation" *(60:18)*. Paul gave a lead: "He hath broken down the middle wall of partition between us" *(Ephesians 2:14)*. A modern analogy has given a technique: in order to break the sound barrier we must reverse the controls. And a needy person has pointed out a successful way—"Let go, let God."*

The pilgrim to Holy Island must treat resentment like the quicksands and the tides. He or she must take heed and give thought; and must let the Holy Spirit of forgiveness make resentment disappear, like one of The Farnes at high tide.

O God, restorer of the years we have destroyed, help us to build up and not tear down. Where a word is sharp on our tongue, withhold it. When an inner sarcasm finds outward expression on our countenance, wipe it off. Make us firm but gentle and so fill our lives with good relationships.

*Attributed to E. Stanley Jones.

Passiontide Begins

LENT—PASSION SUNDAY

Reconciliation's Aftermath

S<small>T.</small> C<small>UTHBERT</small>, the best loved of Northumbria's early
churchmen, is the one most often associated with
Holy Island. This onetime shepherd boy spent many years
as a humble hermit. Islanders still spin stories of his
devout life: how he often prayed for hours while standing
up to his neck in the cold sea water; how he continued
long in acts of penance and self-mortification; how he
retired frequently for meditation to the small island called
now by his name; and how he loved the birds which
flocked to the islands. St. Cuthbert's body, so the islanders tell, was moved from tomb to tomb, at last "to sleep no
more within the sound of the choristers and the music of
the sea." But through his life ran the songs of the Psalter
which brought him joy.

The Psalter has sung its way into the hearts of Jews and
Christians alike, and the songs attributed to David have
become the songs of the ages. Formal worship nearly
always includes one or more psalms read or sung, and this
is a custom long established, going back to the Temple
worship in Jerusalem.

In church, while the Psalter is being read, we are often
arrested by a verse which we want to stop and think
about. But the responsive reading rolls on relentlessly and
usually the verse is forgotten, unless we can remember to

snatch a pencil stub from pocket or purse or cassock and note the psalm for the day so as to return and reflect on its meaning at leisure.

There is one verse, however, which always hits me hard each time this particular psalm is read, and it is difficult to escape from its bald statement, so typical of the uninhibited writers of the psalms. "But I was sore troubled: I said in my haste, All men are liars" *(Psalm 116:10)*. Once while flying across the country I overheard a conversation which took place between a soldier and his seat companion about the break-up of the soldier's marriage. His story ended with this bitter judgment: "I will never trust another woman."

Hearing words of such embittered disillusionment with all people and all life because of an experience with one person and one life, brings to mind many similar experiences of greater or less degree, quite common among us; and this verse of a psalm could be descriptive of such a situation: "I said in my haste, All men are liars."

The author of this psalm speaks for that soldier and many others when he calls *all* men liars and cheats, because *some* of them have been false to him and have disappointed or failed him. But note how honest this unknown writer is as he makes an excuse for his wholesale condemnation: "But I was sore troubled," or perhaps he was just plain "sore." And note, also, how he learned his lesson and found the answer to his condition, which he described earlier in the psalm—when "the pains of hell gat hold upon me . . . then called I upon the Name of the Lord: . . . I was in misery, and he helped me" *(116:3-4, 6)*.

Only God *can* help those who are in such plights, and the moment they believe this and act upon it they are able to swallow and keep down the ashes of bitterness. For it is when such a blow strikes that some lose faith in mankind and others lose faith in the Church and even in God—usually because their faith is so shaky and loosely held in the first place. In this weakened, unbalanced, bewildered, stunned, or hurt condition, men often lash out at life and people, or they withdraw into a shell and refuse to try ever again another experience of living and working with other people, all because of just one moment and one person who failed them and God at the same time. And they never cease saying in haste, "All men are liars."

Speaking with such haste indicates that we are too quickly hurt and much too quickly judge. Regardless of whether we are on the giving or receiving end of such hurt and judgment we find our amazingly fertile minds can dig up excuses for our conduct, whatever it is, and give a reason, no matter how wrong, which eases our mind and conscience temporarily. The Church or Christians or "all men" *en masse* are never at fault, however. The cause of disillusionment really lies in individuals who distort the truth and alter facts to suit their purposes, and so produce the factors which make the unsolved problems of life.

What we need to remember at all times and to relate our thinking and acting to, is that *Christ* is Lord and Master, and not any one human being who happens to block off the truth, causing others to be "sore troubled" or just plain "sore." And to note another point in this psalm, that for one to *cause* even one moment of disillusionment in another is to break the baptismal vow "to continue Christ's faithful soldier and servant unto his life's end."

O Master, walk with us today. O Lord of the day and night, be Lord over every hour of our days and our nights. Lead us by the cloud of thy presence while it is day; and

*when the night comes, pierce our darkness by the light of
thy continued nearness. May our trust in thee not fail and
may we walk unafraid.*

FIFTH MONDAY

See Both Sides

ONE of the major tasks of Christian education is to teach
parents, children, and other individuals to face occasions
of shock and disappointment which come repeatedly to
all, with Christ's kind of magnanimity, forgiveness, and
understanding, and to look at both sides of every
situation—"my" side and the other side. We must learn,
as early and quickly as possible, that in this life we cannot
always count on someone to smooth things over by a
superficial chuck under the chin.

A few parents and children in one parish had a wonderful opportunity to practice this Christian teaching just
before the children's big service of the year, the candle-
light carol service on Christmas Eve. Several eager choristers who had been unable to attend the required weekday
rehearsals for one reason or another, showed up and were
vested. Just before the procession formed, these few
children were told they could not sing in the choir because
of the attendance-at-rehearsal rule. Although this should
have been done when the children first arrived, and
although the parents and choristers should have been
more familiar with the rule, nevertheless the situation
developed as related.

This could have been a heartbreaking experience. Both
parents and children could have met the situation by

rebellion and hurt and unyielding hearts. But after the initial disappointment, the Christian way prevailed. There was no fixing of blame, but an earnest attempt to see *both* sides of the incident which arose because of misunderstandings on *both* sides. All of those children who were left out were in the choir the following Easter Sunday, well rehearsed, singing mightily and joyfully, "Jesus Christ is risen today." They had learned the hard way.

Christian education in Church School and at home attempts to be redemptive; it therefore encourages and teaches children to see as objectively as possible both sides of every question and situation, as Christ taught, rather than to fix blame, to hold grudges, and to retard reconciliation. The Christian's job is to keep on growing in spiritual stature, and forgiveness is part of that growing, one answer to the prayer "forgive us as we forgive others."

Actually, in all such issues we are deeply involved in theology, in this case the Christian doctrine of man, which remains the only realistic way to explain our conduct. No one is sinless except Christ. Through him we have our inner need for purity and forgiveness satisfied and we know the meaning of God's merciful kind of love. Only by his coming to us and continuing with us are we *able* to forgive such incidents as the disappointed choir members and the disillusioned soldier husband. Only by Christ's coming into our hearts and staying there *can* we meet disappointment positively and let nothing remain to fester inside which blocks off God and others, which sours life, and which makes all concerned utterly miserable.

It should be obvious that the business of Christians, those at one with Christ's purpose for life, is not to nurse hurts and wrongs, but to *work* at the *ministry of reconciliation.*

Rethink, then, and reconsider whatever experience still rankles within you and causes distrust of the human race, because of one person who failed you and God, and whom you failed, too, because of your reaction. No one of us is perfect. That is why we need a Savior.

In that stirring hymn, "The Son of God goes forth to war," dedicated to the first Christian martyr, there is a line telling how St. Stephen followed his Master Jesus Christ and "prayed for them that did the wrong." Hard upon this line is the unanswered question, "Who follows in his train?"

Help us to remember, O Lord, that this is the day thou hast made and that we can rejoice and be glad in it; a day made for us to live fully, not waste; a day given for us to use, not spoil; a day to walk through and bring happiness to those we brush past. O Lord, our God, help us to make the most of this day for thee.

FIFTH TUESDAY

No Hasty Utterance

THE unhappy psalmist who said in his haste, "All men are liars," had not Christ. Christians today have Christ, and this makes all the difference. Take, therefore, each peculiar situation and be open to the healing, restoring ministry of his presence in that situation. God will wipe out the past, as we in sorrow confess it, through Jesus Christ, who is both Lord and Savior, and who comes to all hurt and disillusioned ones. He alone can bring true comfort and peace: not a flabby comfort; not an uneasy peace, which makes us weaker and still unsure; but the stretching, sustaining comfort and peace which keep us growing toward his size for us, which is much bigger than we are at present.

Every service of worship in God's house ministers to those who hug their bad experiences in human relations, refusing to be completely honest with themselves or to make any allowances whatever except for themselves. Yet all through each service runs the theme of remembrance of our salvation in and through the crucified and risen Christ, and we are continually reminded of our sinfulness and the loving mercy and forgiveness of God. For example, no one can really pray unless he is willing to deal with the inner condition of hurt and rebellion, whether it be recent or of long standing. In the Collect for the First Sunday after Easter, we acknowledge the fact that God has given his only Son to die for our sins and to rise again so that we may live by faith in him; and we pray, "Grant us so to put away the leaven of malice and wickedness, that we may always serve thee in pureness of living and truth." What greater wickedness than to judge all because of one; what greater truth than to know that all of us have a loving Savior?

We can and do say with the disillusioned psalmist, "All men are liars," but after we have pondered the statement awhile as Christians, we usually admit we, too, were a bit hasty and declare that "all men," even liars, can have Christ as their Savior.

May this be one petition of the pilgrim's litany on Holy Island: "From all hasty utterances of impatience; from the retort of irritation and the taunt of sarcasm; from all infirmity of temper in provoking or being provoked; from love of unkind gossip, and from all idle words that may do hurt, save us and help us, we humbly beseech thee, O Lord" *(The Southwell Litany).*

Dear God, help us to find our way out of the past into thy way of forgiveness and love. Help us to be honest and to make the directions of our days conform to what we know of thee in Jesus Christ our Lord, in whose Name we pray and in whose Way we would walk.

FIFTH WEDNESDAY

The Life of the Fellowship

THERE is a well-preserved Norman doorway to the ancient Priory on Lindisfarne which invites all to enter and find new life, even among the ruins. That gateway to new life might well be labeled, "The life of the fellowship," and the invitation to enter, "Draw near with faith." Once the pilgrim goes through the gateway, he or she beholds the rainbow arch which still stands and is a graceful and beautiful symbol of God's promise, "Lo, I am with you always" *(Matthew 28:20).* This promise of his to the fellowship—which commemorated his death, resurrection, and ascension by "continuing daily with one accord in the temple, and breaking bread from house to house" *(Acts 2:46)*—is still valid.

The life of the fellowship is a continuous performance, beginning back in the first century and still going. It is not like a freshman's experiment in physics, of rubbing one's hand on a piece of fur and then touching metal, which produces a beautiful spark, but only one spark per rub. It is, rather, like the life of a family, lived out together day by day, growing in interdependence and in mutual love, each member helping to fulfill the life of every other member.

Since the life of the fellowship for most Christians is lived out in the parish family, we need to ask, "What is a parish?"

Dr. John Heuss, the late rector of Trinity Church in New York City, made an attempt to be concrete about the true work of a parish, in contrast to the usual limited, feeble expression of this purpose as evidenced in some parishes. He said that "the constant parade of trivialities which the typical church program offers to the public . . . are only rarely related to the real issues which are clawing the soul of modern man to shreds." This should set all Christians thinking about what the God-given functions of a parish really are, and to take a look at their own parish churches in the light of them.

What is a parish? It is a small fragment of the Body of Christ, a one-celled unit of the Christian fellowship. The parish is the whole Christian Church in miniature, "the little church in your house and mine" *(Romans 16:5),* manifesting all the marks of the Church which were laid down in the first primitive attempts at forming a local congregation. "And they continued stedfastly in the apostles' doctrine and fellowship." One parish, for example, is set down in the midst of a great city containing some 8,200,000 souls, with over half of them still to be won for Christ. The Christian mission of this parish to these millions deals with "two entities more important than any nation or all of them: God, and a human being's soul." And the unit through which God is mediated to the human soul is just such a local parish church, and its members. Every parish and every Christian is the Church in "this place," and must bear witness of these things.

It is in the story of the Ascension, as related in *The Acts of the Apostles,* that the faithful are given their marching orders as members of the Christian fellowship. "Ye shall receive power, . . . and ye shall be witnesses unto me" *(Acts 1:8).* And those who heard returned to Jerusalem and began to carry out his plan.

"Ye shall be witnesses unto me." That is what a parish still is for.

This all sounds wonderful and dramatic, and Christians are prepared to believe it is the task to which they have been called as his disciples. But then the business of carrying out Jesus' command falls to them and they falter, and all too often make a sorry mess of it.

The Church, which is often described as a hospital, contains too many patients who fail to get well. The Church, often described as a school, contains too many pupils who fail to learn. Is this, then, the Church's witness to the world, sick and ignorant disciples who know not the Christ whom they claim as Lord? Should churches then close the hospital and school and go out of business? No, for "ye shall be witnesses unto me." The Christian Church has, fundamentally, only one thing to give this torn and harried world: Jesus Christ. It is from him we get, and then share, such essential things of life we cannot manufacture or buy: a Christian sense of humor and perspective; Christian courage, intelligence, and faith; and hope in the eternal purposes of God. We are all ultimately dependent on God who made us, and we are responsible to him for all we think, say, and do. We are indeed his witnesses.

Men are often disillusioned by the conduct of those

labeled "Christians," which is many times shockingly contrary to the ideal of one who is supposed "to follow Christ." This not only causes outsiders to remain outside, but causes some of those who come into the Church with a shining faith to fall away. The only way we can show forth Christ and bear witness to his life is to live as a Christian, work as a Christian, think as a Christian, speak as a Christian, be a Christian parent, boss, and friend, and in all our relationships make real these words from an old hymn, "The touch of his hand on mine."

"Ye shall be witnesses unto *me*."

Give us courage, O God, to admit when we've been wrong, to make restoration no matter what the cost to pride, and to seek from thee the way to do it. Let not the word or conduct of another control us or entice us to words and actions we'll regret. Keep us remembering to find and clean out the rotten places in our lives, so that we shall not have to confess and restore so often; in the name of Christ.

FIFTH THURSDAY

Stumbling Blocks

WE have all been guilty of putting stumbling blocks in the path of another instead of exercising the ministry of reconciliation. When anyone fails to relate what they believe to what they are or can be, the Spirit of Christ is not made manifest in them. When we hear the words of "The Invitation" at the Service of Holy Communion, about being in love and charity with one's neighbors, and accept them and then go away and engage in unloving talk or action, this is treason to the Church and the failure of Christian discipleship.

Do the organizations and activities of the parish to which you belong show forth Christ? The members of the Body of Christ must let everything be done to God's glory and to their own spiritual growth. All the activities of individuals and groups in the parish in some way must become ministering and healing actions, making Christ known at every meeting, in every program and activity. Every Christian always needs to ask, "Is it me, O Lord, standin' in the need of prayer?"

Someone enunciated this truth, "that self-righteous people are hard and blind and that relationships can be maintained only as we are able to forgive because we, too, need forgiveness." Be quick to see and apply this truth, and never overlook it when you pray the Lord's Prayer. The Christian's God-given task is reconciliation, for have we not so known Christ? As members of any fragment of Christ's flock, we must do all we do in the parish to the glory of God, whether it be money-raising, renovating of buildings, sewing, table-setting, or ushering. There is only one way to measure Christian conduct and activities—by the Spirit of Christ. Do some measuring, then, and make it personal, beginning with "me."

Surely the wrongs of violence and bigotry and ignorance and neglect in cities and nations of the world must be righted, and the churches must do all in their power to help by speaking up for the truth and holding before the world the meaning of the Kingdom of God on earth. The churches must work within a responsible society, ministering swiftly and adequately to all human need.

But for most Christians the Kingdom is advanced or retarded by how they act as members of parish groups, how they serve on committees and arrange programs; whether when they speak the truth they do so in love, and when they disagree they do so in the spirit of Christ, and when trying situations arise they do not lose control but exercise patience. Whatever Christians do and the way they do it reveals their concept of the ministry placed in their hands by Christ; and so they are his witnesses, or they are not.

Jesus spoke often about doing "the works of him that sent me." If there be oneness with Christ in the Christian fellowship, all members shall be doing "the works of him that sent me." This is what God wants most from us, to do his work, so we may know of his greatness and goodness, as we interpret and show his love in our words and actions.

The ministry of a parish, then, is not only the inspired and inspiring ministry of music, and the beautiful orderly services, but the personal commitment of each member of Christ's Body to the "Bounden Duty" assigned when the newly confirmed was made a member of Christ's Church—"To follow Christ, to worship God every Sunday in his Church; and to work and pray and give for the spread of his kingdom."

Living and working together as brethren in Christian love, by God's help, just about covers the manner of life set for members of a parish church who are quite literally obeying Jesus' final earthly command to "be witnesses unto me," with the promise of God's power. All parishes are parts of the Body of Christ, and the life of each segment of the fellowship must be lived near him, with his life at the center of its life.

Holy Island today is tranquil without being dull. In the far past, when the stone fragments stood complete in glory, the monks worshiped God and sang his praise, and the sacrament of his life was kept at the heart of the monks' life. Holy Island also had its parish church, and still does, but it was and is apart from the ruins of any past. A Christian parish ministers to its community and its world as a living organism, filled with the power of God, working the works of him who sends us all forth to serve him after they have worshiped him. God's Word, Christ, is the lighthouse which will guide members of any parish fellowship over the shoals and shallows.

If disappointment comes our way this day, good Lord, turn it into blessing and let us learn from it. Let it be a warning not to covet too much for self alone, and let it act upon our hearts without leaving scars of bitterness; in Christ's name.

FIFTH FRIDAY

God's Christ

On Holy Island, the stems of the fossil sea lily, known locally as St. Cuthbert's beads, are sought zealously by the islanders and visitors. These beads are found by working on hands and knees in the sand, turning over tiny shells and other jetsam. As with pearls, it may take the seeker years to secure the right sizes and number to make into a graded necklace.

A lot of time has been spent this Lent in searching for small blessings on Holy Island, for spiritual victories, insights, joys, glimpses, directions, and other beads to string upon the pilgrim's new and more dedicated way of life; and pilgrims marvel over each day lived consistently and rewardingly, which they are able to add permanently as a bead to their character and memory.

Time spent on Holy Island opens our eyes wider to many things, especially the need for greater personal discipline and commitment, and the need for rethinking certain aspects of our Christian faith. But unless we behold and possess the life offered to us by Jesus Christ, who is the center of any Holy Island, we will still be lacking. So turn and look beyond the testimony of his earth-living and dying to his promise of "forever with us."

Man has said, "I believe in God," ever since he built his first altar, which set him forever apart from the other creatures. Most people *do* believe in God. There is something in us which makes us eternally dissatisfied with ourselves and our kind alone. We want something outside ourselves to hold to, and know God is that something. But who is God?

The Bible is the great source book about God, and a faithful record of man's developing idea of God. But even in the Bible we find the Eternal God being slandered and being given the weaknesses of men. Early in the Bible he is described as inconsistent, vindictive, warlike, and jealous, a tribal God. Later on, however, the prophets described him as just, wise, full of loving-kindness, a good and dependable God. But even though many things were learned about him throughout history, a great gap still existed which had to be bridged before man in his finiteness could fully understand the length and breadth of God's kind of love, and the plan which he desired men and women as their own free choice to follow. From the beginning of our reaching after God we sensed there was a *Way* that led to *Life.* But how was it possible for God, who is infinite, to get across to finite persons a living, clearly marked map of the road?

A story may start one toward an answer. A distinguished professor was having an intellectual struggle over the meaning of Christ's life, the reason for it; he did not believe Christ was sent by God. One day as he pondered the problem, a bird flew into his study. It grew panicky when it found itself so confined, and almost exhausted itself in frenzied efforts to beat a way to freedom through a closed window high up under the eaves. The compassionate professor did everything that was *humanly* possible to show the bird a way out, but he failed. Suddenly the thought came to him, "Why, I would have to become a bird before I could ever help this sparrow find the open window. It could only understand my motive and desire for its good if I were one with it." Through this simple experience and conclusion, we see the meaning of Jesus Christ and the reason for him—to show us the way out of our prison house of error, sin, futility, and death. God had the audacity at a definite moment in history to come to us at last as a *Person,* and thenceforth we have known what God is like and what he desires of all; and we have called him Savior.

At one of the evening forums in a religious emphasis week at an eastern college, a Jewish girl asked, "What more of God do you as a Christian possess than we, as Jews?" The speaker reminded her of the story of Madame Curie's search for radium: how she believed in its existence, could measure its tremendous energy, knew where

112

to find it; but only after long years of sacrificial labor, sustained only by her *faith,* did she at last produce a mere smudge in the bottom of an earthen dish which flashed its message out of the darkness, and Madame Curie could say and prove, "*This* is radium." Just so, through the long weary years men believed in God, knew where he might be found, felt his power, but could never really see him until at last there flashed out of the darkness of the ages a light which was Christ; and all could say and prove, because of what he was and did, "This is God—*He* is God"; we could say for the first time "come and see," and point to Jesus Christ. Even though his years were few on earth, Christians believe his Spirit remains as an indelible imprint nevermore to be erased or forgotten, but ever ready to release the power of God and change the lives of us all.

Dear Father, enrich the areas of our confinement, whether they be the narrow limits of a hospital bed or the even narrower limits of a closed mind. Grant us new discoveries of spirit as we allow thee to lead us across barriers of space and time and prejudice, and new dimensions of heart as we grow more patient with those who would minister to us or teach us; in Christ's name.

FIFTH SATURDAY

Christ Is God

No longer must we struggle endlessly to explain about God, to conjure up what he is like. We simply look at Christ and say, "God has shown all of himself in Jesus Christ that we are capable of seeing," and it is enough. We have this treasure—oneness with God through Christ, and it was for us all and for our salvation that he came.

Canon B. H. Streeter of Oxford, whose research and brilliant studies aided our grasp of the truth in the New Testament, wrote many books about God and Jesus Christ, but only when he discovered *The God Who Speaks,* the title of one of them, was his life different and powerful in Christian witness. This dignified scholar, at last, despite his earlier quest for the historical Jesus, found the reality of Christ's presence in his own life. He found the living God in a man, Christ Jesus, and life was ever after more wonderful, because he began to live under his laws and his will.

Yes, most of us believe in God. But it is of the utmost importance for us to believe in God as he really is, rather than in a distortion of him. It is important for us to realize that Jesus Christ is like God, *is* God; that he is the only true and complete picture of the Eternal God; that he is the Mind, the Spirit, back of the universe. He tells us that love is what God wants us to choose, not hate; that humility is God's way instead of arrogance; and that magnanimity is better than pettiness. These are eternal values, established by God and taught by his Son. Whether we like them or not, there they stand. They make up a picture of God and his will for us all. If anything is added or subtracted, the result is a caricature. What is God like? He is like Jesus Christ. Therefore, the most important questions for those who "believe in God" to answer are: "Whom say *ye* that I am?" and "Lovest *thou* me?"

Just think of the wonder and the power and the glory of it! He is caring for all men supremely, loving them limitlessly, forgiving them understandingly, desiring them eternally, and patiently attempting to show them the more excellent way—the way that truly leadeth unto Life! "No man cometh unto the Father, but by me" *(John 14:6)*. "He that hath seen me hath seen the Father" *(John 14:9)*. "I and my Father are one" *(John 10:30)*. No wonder Jew and Gentile alike sought him and cried, "We would see Jesus" *(John 12:21),* because in him we see God manifested in as full measure as we can behold and dare to encompass.

In Jesus Christ is found the God in whom we believe; and it is to him the pilgrim turns on Holy Island, and seeks to place him in the midst of life.

Dear Lord, we know that this day has come from thee to be lived for thee—all of it, every hour, minute, and second of it. We accept thy gift and treasure it, but we need thine aid to live it fully and worthily. We ask that at any moment when our movement is slowed by a solid wall of frustration within or without, thou wilt lead us along the wall until we find a door; for Christ's sake.

VI LENT—PALM SUNDAY

Sorrow's Comfort

THERE is a castle on Holy Island on top of Beblowe Crag overlooking the North Sea, erected as a fort in the sixteenth century to protect the mainland of Northumbria against border raiders. The good men who made the island of Lindisfarne holy would have declared the ruined castle (now restored and lived in) a mute witness to the futility of such secular defense against both barbarian invaders and spiritual evil. They would have pointed instead to Longstone Island's tern-haunted lighthouse, which was built to warn seamen of the dangerous rocks lying jagged beneath the water's surface; and these holy men would have reminded us all of the constant danger of the temptations below the surface of life, declaring the lighthouse a better symbol of the right kind of faith which warns, protects, and guides, than the castle.

Invasion of some kind is always imminent in every life. Take uncomforted sorrow as an ever-present threat to peace of heart and mind. The temptation to sorrow endlessly is one of the weak and vulnerable spots of defense on the mainland of life. The concept of a Holy Island was designed for offering the sufficient strength of God for handling all sorrow. A true story will partially illustrate this.

Once upon a time there was a little girl who had a great

big doll. It was a beautiful doll with a china face, real hair, and eyes that closed; and it was dressed in the finest lavender silk. The little girl loved her doll with a possessive and passionate love. She treasured it above every other thing she owned. One day she was sitting in the back yard watching a ball game one of her brothers had arranged for the neighborhood, with her doll resting snugly in her arms.

All went well until her oldest brother swung at a ball, missed, and let the bat slip out of his hands. It flew over and hit the precious doll squarely on the head, breaking the fragile china to bits. Mary wept bitterly over the loss of her doll. Her brother did his best to tell her how sorry he was, that it was an accident, that he'd save his money and buy her a new doll. But to Mary the loss was irreparable. It was impossible to repair the doll's head and no new doll could ever take its place. No word could comfort the sorrowing child.

The ball game was spoiled and a pall hung over the household until father came home. He realized wisely that there was only one thing to do, although he would willingly have given anthing or done anything to assuage his child's grief. He said little, but took her in his arms and held her close to him until the sobs ceased at last and the tears were finally dried. He knew that soon or late the hurt would heal, even though the memory of it remained; that soon other tasks and other toys would ease the great burden of loss. But for the moment all he could do was hold her in his arms. Healing and comfort for the child came from the father's understanding sympathy, his intense desire to share her sorrow and take it away; the healing power of his love touched her and did its work within her "broken" heart. A good father does care for his children. He loves them, and his arms around them are the outward and visible sign of this love.

We have learned from Christ that God is the good Father who comforts his children in the midst of sorrow, when they allow him. Jesus told how God knows and cares about every sorrow one goes through, how he will wipe away all tears. That is why those who believe him and believe in him do not wail out in agony the eternal *Why?* and break their hearts over a mystery. Nor do they indulge in an orgy of bitterness, cursing God for their loss and hurt. They don't know why sorrow has come. They don't really need to know, for they know him, and know that somehow he will make it all right.

There are many ways of reacting to sorrow and suffering: by self-pity; by a stoical "bloody but unbowed head" philosophy; or by resignation, "it's the Lord's will, so be it." These are distortions of the Christian attitude. But even Christians ask sometimes, Why doesn't God spare his children sorrow?

There is no explanation of suffering and sorrow offered in the New Testament, but it is made clear that God has identified himself fully with human suffering, has gotten into sorrow as deeply as possible, thus enabling us to face it fearlessly and to walk through it by his help. God gave his only-begotten Son to suffer at the hands of the wicked. They, too, are part of his gone-astray creation. How he must suffer over their perversities. "Behold, and see if there be any sorrow like unto my sorrow" *(Lamentations 1:12).* God chose not to be exempt from sorrow and suffering. He still suffers because of us; yet he ever comforts us when we weep in sorrow or wince in pain, and bring both to him. In the New Testament, calamity is taken as an opportunity and turned into a testimony for God. It is not something to escape from; instead, one is to use it because God is there, too. Part of the Good News of the Gospel is that suffering and sorrow are met and overcome, and a way of life is blazed through them by God's oneness with us in them. This is the Christian way of victory over these things, although it may be a slow journey of growth, in time, rather than a quick miracle. Christ is identified with our suffering in every age, and that is how it can be borne.

"Blessed are they that mourn; for they shall be comforted" *(Matthew 5:4)*. Mourners who believe in God *shall* be comforted. The very word *comfort,* taken literally, means "strengthened by being with." The companionship of God is better than a "vein of iron," and we gain exquisite comfort from the fact of the presence of the Father who knows, understands, and shares all. "Come unto me, all ye that travail and are heavy laden, and I will refresh you" *(Matthew 11:28)*.

There is a story told of an old Negro woman whose people were all dead. She lived alone. Asked one day who lived there, she replied with radiant countenance, "Me and Jesus." The Negro Spiritual expresses it rightly; "Nobody knows the trouble I've seen—Glory Hallelujah." Blessed are those in sorrow who believe in him, for they have opened their hearts to receive God's comforting and sustaining presence.

Sorrow melts hard hearts and brings us to God in utter dependence; and we cling to all we know of him through Jesus Christ, until our minds and hearts are at peace. "Yea, though I walk through the valley of the shadow of death . . . thou art with me." *(Psalm 23:4)*. "If I ascend up

120

into heaven, thou art there: if I make my bed in hell, behold thou art there . . . even there shall thy hand lead me, and thy right hand shall hold me" *(Psalm 139:8-10)*. Sorrow, which no one else can assuage, we bring to God through Christ.

For the power to move, we thank thee; for the ability to move from place to place and find new wonders, for the seeing eyes, which can move near and far and all around, for the closeness to all parts of the world by flight in space or of imagination. For a whole, wide world to live in, we thank thee, O God, and rejoice over every moment of living in it.

MONDAY IN HOLY WEEK

No Troubled Hearts

ONLY when a violin string is bound to the instrument, and drawn tighter and tighter, is its purpose fulfilled. It is really free only when it is stretched tautly to the frame and tested; only then can it be tuned to sing its sweetest song. Something like this was meant when a famous singer once said of a young artist, "What a wonderful voice she would have if something would break her heart." It would be too easy for a loving God to spare us and make us spoiled darlings, as some parents do their children, good for nothing. Character and maturity come only by loving firmness.

When a bone is broken, the whole body rushes to the rescue. This is true for an infection; it is also true for "broken" hearts and diseased minds. In much the same

121

way God marshals the inner resources of our souls so that they can be strengthened to stand strong in the face of all adversity. Jesus said from the Cross at the most excruciating extremity of human need, "My God, my God . . . ," and that was his comfort and his strength. Through experience and knowledge of God's comfort in sorrow, there is a bond between all who mourn. Sorrow borne gives the capacity to make others strong in time of weakness, and we share what we have learned: that tears bring a release from spasms of grief and help wash the hurt away; that we can never escape sorrow or suffering, or hide from either, but must meet them, and, as we do, our souls are enlarged to bear whatever comes; that dependence upon God keeps us from self-centeredness and self-pity and releases us from morbid bitterness; that sorrow and suffering can bring people closer to God—"the great sorrows of death and personal loss [likewise the little sorrows] make us quiet, make us listen," some of us for the first time, and his voice brings assurance; that sensitiveness to the needs of others in sorrow comes through our own sorrows. Sorrow and suffering are great teachers for his disciples who are willing learners.

Jesus was a man of sorrows and acquainted with grief. As comforter and comforted he could say, "Come unto me, be with me in God's presence where I have found comfort." Because of him no one need suffer alone, and through him God suffers with his world.

Jesus taught many things, especially the vast meaning of "Our Father." He reminded us of the mourner's eventual happiness beyond shock, numbness, and sharp sense of loss, and he promised never to leave us comfortless. "Let not your heart be troubled: ye believe in God . . ." (John 14:1) who cares for you and whom you can trust no matter what happens. Sorrow does test our faith in God the Father, but when we learn to trust him completely, God deals adequately with every sorrow. God is life and therefore a part of all sorrow. He is in it, around it, above it, and beneath it. He holds us in his arms as fathers hold their own children, and he longs to make all sorrow his own. Truly "underneath are the everlasting arms" *(Deuteronomy 33:27),* in the sense that his presence gives us a feeling of reality and security when adversity comes. In time of sorrow the greatest need is to relate knowledge of God, and belief in God, to the situation at hand, and then let go of it and let God take over.

The sorrow of a little girl over her broken doll, and comfort for her, is the same as the sorrow of one to whom has come a vaster loss. God the Father holds close all those who let him, until they find release. God loves all his children equally and cares for each one the same, like a good human father with four children who gives not one-fourth of his love to each but all of his love to each child. God doesn't need to divide his love, for God is love.

All who sorrow and suffer, much or little, can come unto him and grieve in his presence, knowing he will dry all tears, ease aching hearts, enlarge and strengthen their souls to bear. He will help the suffering to find sufficient light in the darkness to walk by, for God the Father is always near, through Jesus Christ and his Holy Spirit, to hear, to strengthen, and to bless.

O God, we dedicate this day to brightness. Keep near unto us, that our spirits may be a light to one depressed or lonely. Sweeten our words and soften the tone of our voices. In all our relationships, help us to make manifest illuminating love like thine.

TUESDAY IN HOLY WEEK

Where Each One Fits In

SOMETIMES the longest journey anyone can ever make is the journey from a question mark to an exclamation point. The world has had it millions of question marks about Jesus Christ. But on that first Palm Sunday, at the beginning of a week packed with so much meaning, Jesus forced the choice—accept me or reject me; you cannot ignore me.

The question mark is as hard to erase from some minds as is evidence of the past from Holy Island. That is why it is important to read the Gospel evidences concerning Christ's suffering and death which are gathered together in the Prayer Book for Holy Week, and ponder them in the light of the exclamation point given on that first Palm Sunday when Jesus entered Jerusalem on a colt.

The Gospel story of Holy Week faces men with a choice, which puts them among the crowd pecking away at Jesus, hostile and superior toward him, finally rejecting and killing him; or which puts them in the forefront of the spontaneous, enthusiastic, self-forgetting Palm Sunday crowd crying Hosannas. There was no debate for the latter group, no cautious trial balance before acting; they spread their garments before him with zest and exhilaration, for to them Jesus was no longer a question mark but an exclamation point. The choice: either wave palm branches and cry "Hosanna," believing that Jesus is the Christ, "He that cometh in the name of the Lord" *(Mark 11:9),* and in this acceptance find triumph, victory, and salvation in him; or reject him and get ready to crucify him afresh with no hosannas on one's lips.

And yet this enthusiastic public demonstration on Palm Sunday fizzled out, and five days later the King climbed Calvary's hill alone. The question mark was still there, for the certainty turned to dust when the long awaited Messiah was arrested by Roman soldiers without raising a hand to strike back.

Was it love for him and faith in him which they expressed in waving palm branches and shouting their hosannas? Or was it wishful thinking and the result of crowd hysteria? The expectation of the Messiah, so long unfulfilled, might have been the cause.

Jesus had friends who had chosen his way, acting as a dependable network in Jerusalem, who were alerted to his purposes, acquainted with his mind, and ready to act for his cause. For when the colt was sought by the two disciples the strange directions and the password given by Jesus worked perfectly. They went obediently and untied the colt, and when they were challenged, "What do ye, loosing the colt?" they replied "The Lord hath need of him." "And they let them go" (Mark 11:3, 6). The magic password was "The Lord hath need of him." The colt was yielded by its owner because Jesus' need was given priority without question.

Visits to our Holy Island are necessary whenever the question mark struggles to replace the exclamation point. To be immersed in the very atmosphere of such struggles as took place on Lindisfarne centuries ago, strengthens one's faith. The monks who went out from Lindisfarne to face and conquer a pagan world did not know the "grand strategy" but were certain of Christ's command, "go ye."

The great need was and is for faith in Jesus Christ, proceeding from love. In the Father-Son-Master-Disciple relationship, trust and love are essential, based on the belief that God knows best. There is no room and no time in such a loving relationship for endless argument, or for seeking final proof, questioning the wisdom of God the Father. The attitude that made Lindisfarne a Holy Island, built cathedrals, and provided martyrs, centered in a wholly-given-to-God commitment.

Intelligent people choose, take a stand, line up with the constructive forces of love, kindness, and healing, rather than remain aloof. God asks us all to trust him and to believe in his Son. "This is my beloved Son: hear him" *(Mark 9:7)*. And he asks us to stand with him for the forces of light. "He that is not with me is against me; and he that gathereth not with me scattereth abroad" *(Matthew 12:30)*.

The colt episode on Palm Sunday reminds us that our choice commits us to serve him in faith, placing our time, strength, minds, skills, and hearts at his disposal on a priority basis, without hesitation, without question, and without holding anything back when the word comes— "The Lord hath need of them."

O God, for another day to live and love, we thank thee. May we live for thee in each act of kindness, generosity, patience, unselfishness, control of temper. Where thou leadest may we follow; and, O God, lead strongly so that we may surely follow; through Christ our Lord.

WEDNESDAY IN HOLY WEEK

Part and Parcel of His Plan

DOROTHY SAYERS, in *The Man Born to Be King,* has Jesus say: "I can offer you no proof. I can only say, Here I am; believe in me." Jesus revealed his own choice on Palm Sunday; he accepted the hard truth and then stern reality of Saviorhood, and his choice was set. What about yours?

The flow of the Gospels during Holy Week is swift and deep in the direction of the ultimate choice: acceptance of Jesus Christ the Son of the living God as Savior, or rejection. Christians know the score, or should; and because they are solid in their belief that on their own, without God, they can achieve no ultimate good, they see the need of a Savior. Is this the Gospel you have received? Is he the Christ, *your* Lord and Savior? Are there at least glimmers and intimations which pull you toward eventual acceptance? Or is he still a shadowy substance, a dream not yet come true?

It is dangerous to read the Palm Sunday story in the Gospel of Mark *(11:1-11),* for in it the question mark concerning the saving Person of Christ has been erased forever. Here is the truth revealed at last, that Jesus Christ is the Son of God. Mark's words, poured forth with such courage and conviction, continue to roar like a lion down through the centuries, and they strike with a loud note of triumph on the ears of all who would hear.

The palm branch, often fashioned as a small cross for distribution in churches on Palm Sunday, is the ancient

127

symbol of the first day of Holy Week, cherished as a memento of identification by those who are members of God's army, awaiting his orders, descendants of that crowd which waved palm branches and spread their garments in front of him and cried "Hosanna."

The portentous events of Holy Week are worthy of meditation on Holy Island, until they come alive for the pilgrim and fill him with power and a sure sense of Jesus Christ as living Lord and present Savior, "who for us and for our salvation" suffered death upon the Cross.

The Good News from the Gospels is that God was and is in Christ, reconciling the world unto himself. "Blessed is he that cometh in the name of the Lord; . . . Hosanna in the highest" *(Mark 11:9-10).*

The psalmists often penned the questions of our souls accurately, and this was good news for their day. "When I consider thy heavens, the work of thy fingers, the moon and stars, which thou hast ordained; what is man, that thou art mindful of him?" *(Psalm 8:3-4).* All of us have stood in the presence of such vast mysteries of the universe and have wondered humbly, "Where do I fit into this plan of God's creation?" Christianity has declared the answer. We are God's approach to his world; through us his will is done, or is left undone, as we choose. Jesus Christ has shown that to God every person is important. Only Christianity makes such a declaration for man's supreme dignity and worth; only the Christian Church lays such stress on the individual soul as God's instrument.

God made us in his own spiritual image; that is, he placed in humanity the marks of his nature, his likeness, as a son bears resemblance to his father. He has given us the capacity to know him and to have fellowship with him; he has given us freedom, mind, reason, imagination; he has given us the power to understand ourselves and others; he has given us dignity, worth, responsibility; he has given us a purpose which is one with his own—the production of good, the defeat of evil. When we fail in this, we sin. He has given us even the remedy for our failures—forgiveness of sins through the sacrifice of himself upon a cross, to bring us to our knees, at one with his purpose for us. So there is no need for people to ask, as so many do, helplessly and without any expectation of an answer, "Where do I fit into God's plan for his world?" For each created soul is part and parcel of that plan and can contribute to it.

Bless, O Lord, all the days of our years, especially those of sudden growth or sudden pain. As our youth departs and age comes on quickly, help us to adjust gracefully to the load. Keep us ever close to thee and do thou keep ever close unto us, that no day of any year be wasted. By thy grace help us to live them out with strength and courage; through Christ.

MAUNDY THURSDAY

Faith, Obedience, and Fearless Fellowship

THERE are plentiful and available sources for knowledge of God as Lord of the Universe and therefore accurate and final answers to this question, "Where do I fit in?" The Bible, the Church's testimony, human reason and experience, and Christian witness are all sources for knowledge of God and his plan for us. But we shall never make sense out of this world until we turn to God himself for the full revelation of the purpose of life, and then make a personal venture of faith on what we learn about him, continuing to seek constantly his design and designs for us as minute parts of the whole.

The wonderful story about a child and a jigsaw puzzle map of the world never grows old. Given the puzzle, the child put it together so amazingly fast his parents asked him how he did it. The child replied, "Oh, it was easy, for there was a boy on it." The father of the child had failed to notice that on the other side of the map was a picture of Jesus as a young lad. That is why when a man asks, "Where do I fit into this complicated puzzle of the world's life?" he usually turns to the other side and finds the figure of a Man, like unto every man, and he understands and puts the puzzle together quickly. Christ is that Man, with a cross as his background.

What does God expect of us who believe that Christ is his gift, his answer, to human need and perplexity?

One, God expects us to have *faith* in him because of Christ, and to let that faith in his ultimate purpose of peace and brotherhood, honesty and virtue, and release from the powers of darkness, forever shine through our daily thoughts and doings. He asks of us the outward and visible manifestation of his inward and spiritual grace given unto us. The way we face life makes life; our attitude toward life makes it drab or vital. If we believe God is for us and for everyone, and is working to hold us, through our own choosing, to his heavenly laws for earth life, who can be against us? If we believe God is all in all and that nothing else really matters in the long span of eternal values, nothing *can* separate us from him.

In the woods outside Oslo, Norway, during most of World War II, Bishop Eivind Berggrav was behind barbed wire, a prisoner of the Nazis. But his spirit of faith went unconfined to cheer and give courage to those under stress and persecution throughout his beloved land. In his loneliness God was his strength. In his sacrifice he discovered his niche of witnessing for Christ. His faith was the dominant note of courage needed in the Scandinavian countries then and, since the war, in the World Council of Churches which his leadership helped to spark; and even though he is now dead his faith still shines as "a candle in the house" for Christians to see.

Two, God expects of us *loving obedience.* It is of little use to believe in him and his laws of justice, mercy, and truth unless they form the basis of our conduct. If we love him and believe in him, we shall gladly obey him and serve him in any way he asks. "This is how we can be sure that we know him—by obeying his commands" *(I John 2:3),* and we shall be constantly seeking his directions.

Ordinary people who obey God work miracles. So often, when men ask for directions for getting to a particular destination, they write them down and memorize them thoroughly, but until they follow them and *go,* of what value are the directions? So it is with God's commands. He has sent his Son to tell us his plan for achieving healthy, harmonious human relationships, but they will work *only* when one individual after another begins to live free from resentment, envy, hatred, malice, and all uncharitableness. These are God's own directions, and we can never get to our goal of oneness for the human family until we come to ourselves, are really converted to his way and will, and begin to follow his leading in faith.

131

Three, God expects of us faith and obedience, *loving and fearless fellowship,* and a close working together with others, knowing there is strength in numbers and greater influence in a united front. God does not expect us to face the difficulties and dangers of the Christian adventure on this planet alone, without an earthly fellowship as well as a heavenly. This fellowship is charged with knowing Christ and making him known. This fellowship is charged with its own enlargement and strengthening, a world-wide concern for humanity, love for all God's children, and an immovable stand for righteousness.

Where do you and I fit in? Is there not some answer by now? Paul gave as his answer, "So we, being many, are one body in Christ, and every one members one of another" *(Romans 12:5).* We are important individually and as a whole, for we are single bricks in the wall of God's Kingdom on earth, held together by loving obedience to his laws. The best good news is this: that we and God through Christ are an unbeatable combination. This is the Church, and upon this combination rests God's plan for the redemption of the world. We are called by him to be doers of the Father's work, and will. In so doing we are one with Christ, and the life he called abundant is ours to have and to share. Jesus himself is our certainty. The basis of Jesus' expectations and hopes in us is our answer to his pleading question, "Lovest *thou me?*" On this simple and personal basis we declare ourselves.

Just as God has placed masses of birds on every pinna-cle and ledge of the small island of The Farnes, and in every crevice and chasm of the larger islands, giving to each bird knowledge of its own nesting place and where to lay its eggs, so he grants to us the sure knowledge of where each one belongs, at one with him who made and sustains us all.

O God, we thank thee for life; for its colorful beauty all around—the flowers of the land, the saltiness of the sea, the cleanness of the mountain air, and whatever is sensed that makes life wonderful. May awareness of these things overbalance whatever of ugliness and foulness brushes our senses. Lift our hearts and minds to thee, O God, and keep thou close to us; through Jesus Christ, our Lord.

GOOD FRIDAY

Anticipation of Death's End

WHEN spring comes to Holy Island, the pilgrims there are certain once again that God is not dead, and their attention is focused on an empty Cross, from which light shines to puncture whatever darkness surrounds them. The pilgrims' certainty is augmented by the frenzy of emerging life nature always provides for background, "Earth's shouting of victory, and flinging up its colored cap to the sky."*

On Holy Island the pilgrim never tires of discussing the Resurrection, for it brings reassurance that, though we die, we do not die eternally; and this bolsters our faith that God's roaring loom of time is weaving an enduring fabric of life for living beyond history. We want to shout with Lazarus: "There is no Death; There is only Life: Death is the fear between man's *no* and man's *yes* to God."*

---

*Eugene O'Neill, *Lazarus Laughed,* Random House, N.Y., 1927.

133

Paul spends half the fifteenth chapter of I Corinthians trying to answer the question, "How are the dead raised up?" But to explain *how* the dead are raised up is as difficult as giving exact answers to questions concerning the intricate workings of nature, the fascinating discoveries of science, or even the composing of a symphony.

It would be just as simple to ask, and equally impossible to answer, how does the heart beat or how does the eye see? We could give a word picture of the eye, for example, this unique member of the body, without which man would walk in darkness. We could liken the eye to a camera which takes pictures, colored pictures and moving pictures, without once reloading, and which focuses automatically in any light, at any distance. We could note that it also develops, prints, and files away countless pictures as mental images in a vast "morgue." But when the description is finished we still don't know how such a complex instrument could have been conceived and executed. But it was adequate to do it. Our knowledge, or lack of it, does not affect our seeing. It would be foolish of us, wouldn't it, to say "I don't believe it," just because we can't understand *how* the eye can possibly see?

Or take atom smashing. It is "old stuff" now, but just ask a scientist to explain what happens when an atom is smashed. He will probably say that the atom is not smashed or split at all, that it is transmuted into radiant energy. Atom smashing, which brings to mind an infinitesimal speck disappearing into nothingness, is really a process which releases something the scientists call "radiant energy," and the atom is not destroyed at all, but transmuted, changed from one form to another.

We can describe such miracles as sight and nuclear fission, but we cannot explain them.

So it is with the resurrection life and the question, "How are the dead raised up?" Inconceivable as all this is to our finite minds, we have clung to the faith that continued existence and growth in some form after death are part of God's plan, and in them is the fulfillment of our deep-seated longing for completion.

God has planted within us our longings and our needs. He has also provided the means for satisfying them. The Christian faith declares that God is sufficient to satisfy all human hunger, whether for physical food or for hope beyond the curtain of time, and that we can trust him.

Paul's illustration of the seed dying and bringing forth life in a new kind of body is good, and refers to the spiritual body as well as the physical. "That which thou sowest is not quickened, except it die" *(I Corinthians 15:36).*

We are told that physical matter is never destroyed, but only changes its form, which is its death and resurrection, and no one questions this fact. Is it any less easy to believe that Spirit, which makes fleshly matter vibrant and creative, is not wasted eternally, but changes *its* form, and goes through a similar death and resurrection by God's grace? One of the famous Compton brothers, the physicist, tells us that "Science has found no cogent reason for supposing that what is of importance in a man can be buried in a grave," and he might have added, "forever dead."

O God, we thank thee for another day; for the light and for the promised warmth clear through to our hearts. Be it a lazy day or a busy day, hold us to moments of remembering that thou art near to help and to bless. O God, we thank thee for another day.

EASTER EVEN

In Between Death and Life

EVER since the early Church got its belief straight on the subject of the resurrection of Jesus Christ, it has made its choice of faith in him who gives us the victory over the one certain, supremely tragic, universal, and inescapable fact of death—death of the body and death of soul. The Christian Church states it succinctly on Easter Day: God is not dead, "He is risen"; and the faithful reply, "He is risen indeed." In him, we, both body and soul, are alive.

Note how the practical Paul, in his first letter to the Corinthians, makes a swift change from his discussion of the tremendous experience of life after death, which his hearers had not yet experienced, to a word about the continuing earth-life which confronted them, and which confronts us today, too. He switched from talk about bodily resurrection and how man's natural body would be raised a spiritual body, and how God would give to each his own body, and ended with a great shout of praise— "Thanks be to God, which giveth us the victory through our Lord Jesus Christ. Therefore, my beloved brethren, be ye stedfast, unmoveable, always abounding in the work of the Lord" *(I Cornithians 15:57-58)*.

Paul gave as honest and complete an answer as he could to the question, "How are the dead raised up?" and then urged Christians to live as fully as possible their life span on earth, and leave the rest to God. "Forasmuch as ye know [or ought to know] that your labour [on earth] is not in vain in the Lord" *(I Corinthians 15:58)*.

Easter Day contains the surprise of being loved out of the shadowy darkness of death. And here we move into a different emphasis on death and resurrection, not God's death on a cross and resurrection from a grave, the death of Death, but the death of sinful self and rising to new life. "For whosoever will save his life shall lose it: and whosoever will lose his life for my sake shall find it" *(Matthew 16:25).* "Likewise reckon ye also yourselves to be dead indeed unto sin, but alive unto God through Jesus Christ our Lord" *(Romans 6:11).*

That is why Christians pray, "Grant that we, being dead unto sin, may live unto righteousness, and being buried with Christ in his death, may also be partakers of his resurrection." The fact of resurrection from inner decay, as well as bodily disintegration, saves both earth-life and death from being a mockery.

There are those who walk around in bodies physically alive, yet they act like they are empty and hollow, without animation, with minds, hearts, and souls dragged down to the least possible spiritual effectiveness. This lethargy and paralysis are due to the "sting" of sin, the "no" to God which man tossed off his prideful tongue before darkness set in. The main job on Holy Island is to quicken and arouse the spiritually dead, to strengthen their souls to stand, to bring about a resurrection so that we who appear dead may rise to life, a new life which will be ever expanding on both sides of the barrier of death, and to get us saying "yes" to God.

The Christian Gospel is full of love and hope for all, as Christ taught. Just so long as there is any sign of life in a person or a situation, efforts must be continued to raise us from deadness to life through sermons, work, prayers, love, imposing disciplines, regular trips to some Holy Island, and witness. "His Cross has made possible the forgiveness of our sins. His resurrection can also be our resurrection."

While on earth, Jesus formed an intimate fellowship to teach us how to live his way. But the first response, while significant, was not in the nature of a resurrection to power and full life. It took the Crucifixion *and* the Resurrection to wake us at last from the deadness of our ways and move us toward the full development of our potential life. The Gospel of resurrection is for both "the quick [the living] and the dead"; and though "the wages of sin is death," yet for every one of us "the gift of God is eternal life through Jesus Christ our Lord."

Now to him who can strengthen us by Jesus Christ; who has revealed the secret purpose which after the silence of long ages has now been disclosed and made known on the basis of the Scriptures in the person of his Son; to the only wise God be glory through Jesus Christ for ever and ever (Romans 16:25-27).

EASTER DAY

Risen with Christ

THE shock treatment, used in many cases of mental illness, is not new. It was used on Good Friday. Yet the effect was not fully perceived and felt until Pentecost, the day the Holy Spirit possessed the disciples and waked them at last to the fact they had missed—that the way out of their "hole" of impotence is dying to the demands of self and responding to the demands of God. Jesus Christ presented the demands of God in his very person as he confronted us with the evidence of our own sinfulness in the presence of God. However, instead of being convicted of sin and driven to repentance, we have tried to kill God. The Crucifixion came as a shock treatment, and it is the one effective way today of helping us choose to die to the old self and rise to the new life with God. It is death unto sin which gives resurrection unto life, and the victory is the removal of sin, the "sting" of death.

When we begin to question ourselves as we really are, and catch a vision of what we can become by God's grace, strange and wonderful things happen. The question of bodily resurrection must be up to God, but we can spend our time and energy in overcoming our own spiritual lethargy and refusal to rise from the dead. There is no resurrection without death. There is no spiritual change without rebirth. The seed's life does not quicken except it die to its seed-self in order to fulfil its potential flower-self. So our inner life comes to full flower when our "no" to God becomes "yes."

Christ's coming brought not only the realistic facing of life at every level, but he brought judgment to us in a way it could be accepted. We realize finally it is our sin which led to the Crucifixion and that only by our own death unto sin can there be any resurrection for us; and we are thus enabled to face ourselves as we really are, under the judgment of God, because we are assured of God's love and acceptance of us and that, no matter what our condition, however unloveable we might be, God does love us.

Since God died on a cross and we were shocked into facing ourselves realistically, we have come to realize there is no use pretending. All of us must face what we are

139

in the presence of God and then turn away from our deadness, accepting the forgiveness and love and life which God offers.

The theme of resurrection is familiar to musicians and poets, scientists and historians, Christian zealots and halfway Christians alike. But until the Easter "song of victory" leads to the remaking of life by his life, the yielding to his way for our way, what does it profit us to say, "He is risen," and yet remain grounded and unchanged in the presence of the miracle of God's love and concern for us, still refusing the power of grace made available to us through his Son?

But all this must come home to each one. Each of us must ascend Calvary's hill and die with Jesus Christ before discovering life with him on the road to Emmaus, or finding more of him in sermons, Scripture reading, devotional disciplines, and worship. "If ye then be risen with Christ, seek those things which are above, where Christ sitteth on the right hand of God" *(Colossians 3:1).*

The exciting last notes of César Franck's great *D-minor Symphony* swell to a climax and arouse in the listener inner stirrings of God's presence, furnishing a background against which Paul's words, "how are the dead raised up?" stand out in bold relief and find their answer. Each day of resurrection is truly in the mood of Franck's D-minor music which makes an appropriate new setting for the ancient Easter theme: "Alleluia, he is risen." The symphony plays against the dark background of time and illumines it and fills our souls with the ringingly exuberant truth that God is not dead, that our cruelty has done its worst, but it cannot kill God forever. Because "He is risen," the light is still shining in the darkness, for the darkness can never put it out. Each one can see in the brown, unsightly bulbs, the hidden flower created to bloom there. "That which thou sowest is not quickened, except it die" *(I Corinthians 15:36).*

The Christian faith is in Christ, resurrected and triumphant, in whom is found "radiant energy" for living, and courage and comfort for the crossing in glory from one life to another. Christ loves us all, even when we are most difficult and hideous, and provides the courage, faith, and power for us to win the victory over sin, through dying to self and rising to newness of life.

There are many examples of challenge and response, which lead to the soul's growth, to spiritual resurrection, and to the answers to "How are the dead raised up?" When we reach dead ends, the challenge either kills our spirit or forces us to seek beyond ourselves for finding a way out. This means death or resurrection. When sin snatches away our dignity and power, it either leaves us bereft of hope or forces us to admit defeat of self and ask for help from God—like the alcoholic who either stays in the gutter or accepts the challenge of Alcoholics Anonymous. This is death or resurrection. When God places thoughts in our minds and there is an intense urge to take a step, we either dare to follow the leading with vigor, trusting him who leads, or we falter and in fear shrink away. This is death or resurrection. When some great ideal challenges us, we must either cry, "No, it is too big for me," and leave the response up to another, or be caught by it and push ahead against odds to stir up God's-Kingdom-on-earth life. This brings death or resurrection. When we sicken of the old life because of a vision of better things to be, when we come to ourselves at last,

141

we must either stay with the old life or strike out for God's way, born again spiritually. There must be either death or resurrection.

He is not "here"—only death is here. He is risen. He is where life is. Seek him among the living, growing places of the mind and heart. Yield to his pull down to a good rootage.

Time apart on Holy Island opens our eyes wider to many things, but, unless we pilgrims catch a glimpse of his life offered to us forever, we will still be earthbound. So, finally, we turn and look beyond the living and the dying, and find death's end in Christ.

EASTER MONDAY

Looking Back on Holy Island

AFTER any stay on Holy Island, leave-taking is always to the sound of muted trumpets, for the victories gained apart in the presence of God have been wrested from frequent defeats. As we look back on our visit to Holy Island and what it has meant to us, certain words and phrases and disciplines associated with our stay remain. They are like a string of "St. Cuthbert's beads" worn as a "necklace" around our memories, keeping us encouraged, humble, and convinced the findings were worth the search.

Prayer is one special, shining bead which has been added on our trip to Holy Island, and we have become "bedesmen" (men who pray) for Christ. Holy Island beckons us to pray, to shut ourselves off from the world

142

for a time of quiet with God, for learning more about him and his way; then to return refreshed and better fitted for living once again in the world.

Lent is a Holy Island where we have spent a lot of time searching for small blessings, victories, insights, joys, glimpses, directions, and other "beads" to string upon our new and more dedicated way of life.

Pilgrims might have turned over the sands of time again and again without a "bead," but discovering even one response made, one moment of insight given, one microscopic evidence of inner growth, is a sign of life, is something to hang onto, for all life comes from a single cell, or two cells merged as one, which grow and make two, then many.

The buildings on Holy Island, which were frequented during our Lenten pilgrimage, especially the solemn, huge, and dark-red pile of ruins of the island's Norman Priory, have crumbled since the centuries of St. Aidan and St. Cuthbert and their holy clan. But the spirit of those men, and the hundreds who followed them, lives on and keeps alive Holy Island's other name, Lindisfarne, which means over the river Lindis to a place of retreat. Holy Island exists for the sake of all Christians—for renewing their strength, for recovering from wounds, for growing in grace to overcome the world, in the sense that Christ overcame it. But it also exists as a base of operations for us all, as in St. Aidan's days, where we can come into close contact with the One in command, preparing ourselves to go forth and bear witness to others and bring them to Christ.

The test of any time apart on Holy Island is how well pilgrims handle the pressures and frustrations and irritations of life upon their return. The quietness of such times

143

apart must carry over as a portable island within, with the pilgrims' prayer as a continuing contact. "Bless, O Lord, our new effort to respond to thy love by loving."

In the fragments which remain on Holy Island, the past looms large; but out of the past comes God's promise to be with us always, and the restored parish church on the island bears witness to a continuity of prayer and praise. Because of this past and this continuity we are better able in these days to face solemnly certain basic questions of vital importance to our faith, and to find answers to carry us through, undaunted and unafraid.

Has it been so with you on your visit to Holy Island? Has the reading of this book been a Holy Island? Remember that even in the little exchanges of the social amenities one can witness to the experiences on Holy Island. The citadels of self-will and self-love have been attacked. Have they come down? Has the Christian perfection sought for so valiantly been found where St. John, St. Paul, St. Thomas Aquinas, St. Cuthbert, St. Teresa, St. Augustine, and all the other saints found it, in the life of Christian love in relation to persons? Love is the essence of the transformed life, begun on Holy Island and continued in the life to be lived for him day by day.

So live by God's grace, and "the God of peace be with you all" *(Romans 15:33).*

Now the God of hope fill you with all joy and peace in believing, that ye may abound in hope, through the power of the Holy Ghost (Romans 15:13).